THE
SHAKER
HERB AND
GARDEN
BOOK

THE
GARDENER'S MANUAL;

CONTAINING

PLAIN INSTRUCTIONS FOR THE SELECTION, PREPARATION, AND

MANAGEMENT OF A

KITCHEN GARDEN:

WITH PRACTICAL DIRECTIONS FOR THE CULTI-
VATION AND MANAGEMENT OF SOME
OF THE MOST USEFUL

CULINARY VEGETABLES.

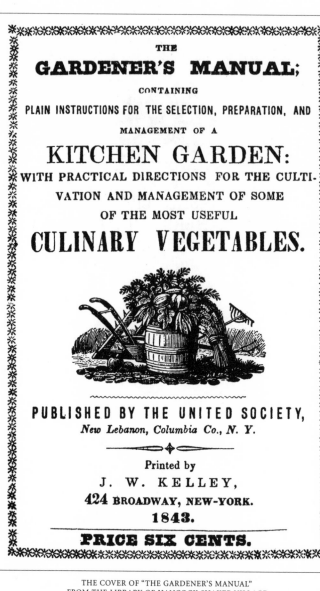

PUBLISHED BY THE UNITED SOCIETY,

New Lebanon, Columbia Co., N. Y.

Printed by

J. W. KELLEY,

424 BROADWAY, NEW-YORK.

1843.

PRICE SIX CENTS.

THE SHAKER
HERB AND GARDEN
BOOK

RITA BUCHANAN

PHOTOGRAPHY BY PAUL ROCHELEAU

DESIGN BY DAVID LARKIN

PUBLISHED IN ASSOCIATION WITH
HANCOCK SHAKER VILLAGE

HOUGHTON MIFFLIN COMPANY

BOSTON NEW YORK 1996

FOR INFORMATION ABOUT PERMISSION TO REPRODUCE SELECTIONS
FROM THIS BOOK, WRITE TO PERMISSIONS, HOUGHTON MIFFLIN COMPANY,
215 PARK AVENUE SOUTH, NEW YORK, NEW YORK 10003.

LIBRARY OF CONGRESS CATALOGING-IN-PUBLICATION DATA
BUCHANAN, RITA.
THE SHAKER HERB AND GARDEN BOOK / RITA BUCHANAN.
P.   CM.
INCLUDES INDEX.
ISBN 0-395-73325-1
1. ORGANIC GARDENING. 2. VEGETABLE GARDENING. 3. HERB
GARDENING. 4. SHAKERS. 5. HERBS — THERAPEUTIC USE. I. TITLE.
SB324.3.B835 1996 03-18-96
635'.08'8288 — DC20   96-11239

PRINTED IN THE UNITED STATES OF AMERICA
QUM 10 9 8 7 6 5 4 3 2 1

PRINTED ON RECYCLED PAPER

FOR INFORMATION ABOUT THIS AND OTHER HOUGHTON MIFFLIN TRADE AND
REFERENCE BOOKS AND MULTIMEDIA PRODUCTS, VISIT THE BOOKSTORE AT
HTTP://WWW.HMCO.COM/TRADE.

Rita Buchanan and Paul Rocheleau thank the staff and associates of
Hancock Shaker Village, particularly Norman Burdick, Bernice Fiske,
Liz Fitzsimmons, Ann Hanchett-Boland, Eric Johnson, Wendy Liebenow,
Sarah McFarland, Andrew Vadnais, Tom Weldon, and Susan Zweig, for
their generous assistance in researching and developing this book.

Production design by Meredith Miller.

The photographs on pages 90, 129, 131, and 142
were taken by Rita Buchanan.

CONTENTS

WHO WERE THE SHAKERS?

Put your hands to work and your hearts to God.
—MOTHER ANN LEE

TO MANY AMERICANS TODAY, the name "Shaker" refers to a style of furniture, as in Shaker table, Shaker mitten box, or even Shaker video center. This is a misunderstanding and a missed opportunity. The people called Shakers did make furniture, but that was not their primary mission. Shakerism was first a religion and second a way of life. The clean design, high-quality materials, and careful workmanship evident in their furnishings are just the most visible reminders of a much broader and deeper system of values and beliefs.

Once you start to learn more about the Shakers, you can't help but be fascinated by their idealism and integrity. These people were passionately committed to improving human nature and building a model society—to living like angels in a heaven on earth. They strived for a perfection that encompassed simplicity, harmony, order, usefulness, efficiency, and beauty—values that many of us appreciate today. When we learn about the Shakers, we are reminded to set our sights high, live up to our beliefs, and not yield to complacency, laziness, or despair.

The Shakers made contributions in many fields, as religious thinkers, social pioneers, craftsmen, inventors, and builders, but they were especially successful as gardeners. In addition to producing their own food, they developed major businesses—the largest and most advanced of their time—selling vegetable seeds and medicinal herbs, which they grew, processed, and packaged themselves. The Shaker approach to gardening is the focus of this book, but to put it in context, I'll start with an overview of Shaker religion and life.

SHAKERISM AS A RELIGION

The Shakers had another name for themselves; they called themselves Believers, or members of the United Society of Believers. They believed that the life of Ann Lee, often called Mother Ann, signaled the second coming of Christ and the beginning of the Millennium, the thousand-year period of goodness and light described in the biblical book of Revelation. Ann Lee was a poor factory worker in Manchester, England, when she started having the visions and revelations that transformed her into a charismatic leader. She began preaching that men and women should confess their sins, renounce lust, and adhere to celibacy. She promised that all those who heeded the call to a pure, Christly life would be united with God and find eternal salvation.

Outsiders gave Mother Ann and her followers the name Shakers or Shaking Quakers because of their form of worship. When the spirit moved them, Ann Lee and the other early Shakers would shake violently, twirl until they dropped onto the floor, shout, moan, throb, and make other impassioned gestures. Early Shaker worship was spontaneous, noisy, and chaotic. Later it became a much more structured routine of silent prayer, spoken messages or readings, group singing, and patterned dancing, but the name "Shaker" persisted long after the Believers stopped shaking, and they willingly accepted the term and used it regularly themselves.

Persecuted for their beliefs in England, Ann Lee and eight of her relatives and followers came to America. In 1776 the group bought land near Albany, New York, and set about building a community for the faithful. The first few years were a struggle, but by the time Mother Ann died in 1784, the movement was already gaining momentum, and new leaders were ready to organize and direct its growth. They wrote down Mother Ann's sayings and ideas (she herself was illiterate), developed rules for membership in the society, vigorously recruited new members, established a chain of authority, and set up an orderly system of communal living.

Shakerism was definitely a form of Christianity, but its tenets differed considerably from orthodox Protestant and Catholic ideas. For one thing, the Shakers didn't consider the Bible as the infallible last word; they were open to ongoing revelation. They denied the concept of original sin and claimed that any person could achieve spiritual perfection by living a pure life. Also they believed that God has both male and female attributes, as expressed through the lives of Jesus Christ and Mother Ann, and that men and women have equal rights and responsibilities. These and other ideas were developed over time by a few key leaders, who published various tracts and books explaining the sect's origins and beliefs.

Average Shakers didn't spend much time thinking about theology. They attended the Sunday meeting for worship and prayed regularly during the week, but much of their religion was expressed through everyday life. In this sense the key points of the religion could be expressed in simple terms. As one Believer wrote:

The nine cardinal virtues of Shakerism are:

1st. Purity in mind and body—a virgin life.

2d. Honesty and integrity of purpose in all words and transactions.

3d. Humanity and kindness to both friend and foe.

4th. Diligence in business, thus serving the Lord. Labor for all, according to strength and ability, genius and circumstances. Industrious, yet not slavish; that all may be busy, peaceable and happy.

5th. Prudence and economy, temperance and frugality, without parsimony.

6th. Absolute freedom from debt, owing no man anything but love and good-will.

7th. Education of children in scriptural, secular, and scientific knowledge.

8th. A united interest in all things—more comprehensive than the selfish relations of husband, wife, and children— the mutual love and unity of kindred spirits, the greatest and best demonstration of practical love.

9th. Ample provision for all in health, sickness and old age; a perfect equality—one household, practicing every virtue, shunning all vice.

SHAKER SOCIETIES

The Shakers clustered in communal societies partly to escape the scorn and prejudice they encountered as religious heretics, but also to benefit by working together, sharing their resources, and reinforcing each other's commitment to their common beliefs. Group living was economical and efficient, and the constant supervision and peer pressure helped keep Believers on the straight and narrow path, apart from the beguiling "World" of non-Believers who indulged in sinful ways.

Between 1787 and 1836, twenty-two Shaker societies or communities were established in New York, Massachusetts, Connecticut, New Hampshire, Maine, Ohio, Kentucky, and Indiana. (In the late 1890s, two more societies were started in Georgia and Florida but were soon discontinued.) Each society owned as much as several thousand acres of farmland and forest, and each built a meetinghouse, dwellings, barns, workshops, mills, office, school, infirmary, and other structures as needed. These local societies were fairly independent; they ran their own businesses, admitted their own members, and solved their own problems, but all acknowledged the authority of the central Shaker ministry at New Lebanon, New York. (In 1861 this community changed its name to Mount Lebanon, but I use New Lebanon throughout the book to avoid confusion.) There was regular correspondence and visitation between the leaders of local societies and between each society and New Lebanon.

To join a society, men or women had to be at least twenty-one years old, had to obtain the consent of their spouse, if married, and had to be free of any debt or obligations. Then they signed a covenant, donated their personal property to the group, agreed to work for the mutual good, and accepted the authority and rules of the order. In return, members received room and board, employment, security, health care, and an equal share in the group's assets. At first the Shakers were able to recruit some well-to-do farmers who donated their land, buildings, tools, and livestock to the society. Later on, most converts had little to contribute.

Each society housed some members who had signed the covenant and made a lifetime commitment; these people provided stability and served as leaders. There were other men and women who were considering membership but were still uncommitted and some who didn't have any intention of joining but simply needed a place to stay for a while. These people earned their keep and sometimes brought practical skills and knowledge to the society, but their comings and goings often caused turmoil. Finally there were children—those of members and tentative converts, others indentured to the society by parents who were unable to care for them, and orphans. The Shakers raised thousands of children in a firm but loving way, put them to work, taught them a skill or trade, and provided a basic education, hoping that when they came of age they would choose to sign the covenant and join the society. This was a reasonable strategy for a celibate society, but in fact most of the children raised by the Shakers left when they grew up— or in some cases ran away sooner. Only a small percentage stayed on to become members.

Socially the Shaker societies were more or less isolated from the World's people, but economically there was constant interaction. The Shakers needed money to acquire land, to pay taxes and legal fees, to buy building materials and tools, to develop and promote their businesses, to recover from fires and other disasters, to pay hired hands when they didn't have enough workers of their own, to enjoy food they couldn't produce themselves, and to buy household notions and supplies. Although thrifty, they didn't hesitate to buy what they needed and to choose the best-quality goods. Earning money was a constant concern that each society faced in its own way by selling whatever they could produce, including garden products, such as applesauce, dried sweet corn, maple sugar, pickles, vegetable seeds, fruit trees, dried herbs, and herb extracts; butter, cheese, and milk; baskets and brooms; chairs and other furniture; and yarn, woven fabric, knitted goods, and other textiles. These products were sold wherever there was a market—locally, regionally, around the United States, and even overseas.

THE SHAKER WAY OF LIFE

Shakerdom was no place for people who valued privacy and autonomy. Daily life was crowded and closely supervised. The basic social group, called a "family," usually numbered from twenty-five to one hundred or more adult "brothers" and "sisters" and unrelated children. Men, women, boys, and girls slept in dormitory-type rooms, separated by sex and age. They all came together for meals and meetings and sometimes in the

11

course of work, but men and women were not allowed to engage in casual, unchaperoned conversation.

Each family was supervised by a "parental" team of two elders and two eldresses, who monitored behavior, imposed discipline, heard confessions, provided spiritual leadership, and made all the executive decisions about the family's projects and activities. Other men and women, designated as deacons, deaconesses, and trustees, were the hands-on managers. They maintained the buildings and grounds, ran the businesses, supervised farm and household chores, bought and sold property and goods, and did the bookkeeping. Furniture, clothing, tools, books, and other objects belonged to the society as a whole and were provided for individual Believers to use. Individuals could not have private possessions, nor were they to keep secret letters, documents, or private thoughts hidden from the elders.

Everyone worked. Jobs were assigned according to ability, aptitude, and the need to get things done. Sisters cleaned all the buildings, did laundry, sewed and knitted, milked the cows and made butter and cheese, processed fruit and vegetables for storage and sale, cooked and baked, served meals, did dishes, and helped with the herb, seed, and other businesses. Brethren did farm chores and cared for the livestock, tended the crops and gardens, made hay, cut firewood, maintained the roads and fences, erected buildings, ran the mills, fixed the machinery, and delivered goods to market. Children labored alongside the adults and also went to school for four months a year— boys in the winter and girls in the summer.

Although everyone worked, some workers were more productive than others. In their journals, the head gardeners frequently complained about the shortcomings of their assigned helpers, who included Aged Brethren (older men with reduced strength and stamina), invalids suffering from physical or mental illnesses who were sent to the garden for therapy, and boys who were too young to work and needed constant supervision. As Franklin Barber wrote in July 1842, "Five of the youngest of the boys in the boys order move from the brick shop to the upper south room in the seed shop. I assist in moving them, fixing the room, etc. It is intended for them to work in the garden and the burden of taking care of them falls upon me, which is not small…the oldest being 9…the youngest 3." Franklin himself was only twenty at the time, and was responsible for the five-acre seed garden at New Lebanon. Years later, when the society was having trouble recruiting and retaining young men, the gardeners had to use hired hands to get the work done.

The scheduled routine varied little from day to day and week to week, with set hours for getting up, eating, working, attending meetings, and going to bed, and no free time for idleness or mischief. However, the gardeners and farmers may have enjoyed more flexibility than most workers, because of the exigencies of weather and the urgency of timely planting or harvest. Sometimes they were even excused from Sunday or weeknight worship services.

The early Shaker leaders had a heightened—you might say exaggerated—concern for order, regularity, uniformity, and tidiness. To standardize the Believers' behavior, they developed the Millennial Laws, first published in 1821 and revised in 1845 and 1860. These laws—there were pages of them—covered most aspects of everyday personal and community life. Some are very practical, others seem petty. Later in the book, I quote several laws that relate to gardening. Here are a few other examples from the Millennial Laws of 1845, to give you a feeling for the Shaker way of life:

> No one should talk while eating, and no one present should talk to any person that is eating, unless it be very necessary....
>
> Slamming doors or gates, loud talking and heavy walking in the dwelling house, should not be practiced by Believers....
>
> No smoking or taking snuff, may be done in the kitchens, and no one may smoke and work at the same time....
>
> No kind of ardent spirits may be used among Believers, as a beverage, nor on any occasion except by order of the Physicians....
>
> Fancy articles of any kind, or articles which are superfluously finished, trimmed or ornamented, are not suitable for Believers, and may not be used or purchased....
>
> When brethren and sisters go up and down stairs, they should not slip their feet...but lift them up and set them down plumb, so as not to wear out the carpets or floor unnecessarily....
>
> All should retire to rest in the fear of God, without any playing, or boisterous laughing, and lie straight.

13

HOW WE KNOW ABOUT THE SHAKERS

The Shakers left extensive written records. They published religious tracts, accounts of their history, biographies and autobiographies, catalogs of products for sale, and a few books of gardening advice and recipes. For their own use, they kept detailed ledgers, account books, and journals. There are also descriptions (both praising and damning) of Shaker life written by ex-Believers who had left the society and by interested outsiders who had visited or lived with the Shakers for some period of time. Still, many details went unrecorded, and there are many gaps in our knowledge. In putting together this description of Shaker gardening, I sometimes had to read between the lines or put two and two together. I raise some questions in this book that I haven't found answers for and perhaps never will. People who study Shaker furniture and architecture have the advantage that those artifacts endure. Gardens disappear.

Of all the historical sources, I think the most fascinating by far are the journals of daily work and events. Throughout this book I quote from the journals of various gardeners. I felt a special kinship with Franklin Barber at New Lebanon because he noted the same kinds of events and ideas in his journal that I write in mine. Unfortunately his tenure as head gardener was brief. In 1844, at age twenty-two, he died of tuberculosis.

Shaker journals were supposed to be strictly businesslike, and in fact the entries are often terse, routine accounts. But sometimes the writers strayed from their assigned topics and gave an uncensored view of Shaker life by commenting on other concerns. They gossiped about other people in the society, complained of being overworked and needing more help, and lamented over accidents, illnesses, deaths, and the loss of members who defected to the World. On the positive side, the journal writers noted special meals such as the first picking of strawberries or a dinner of fresh fish, appreciated the gift of beautiful weather, welcomed visitors who brought news and ideas, and reported on holidays. For example, Philemon Stewart, a gardener at New Lebanon, noted a solemn Thanksgiving and Christmas but a hopeful New Year:

November 26, 1846: This day we have kept as Thanksgiving in prayer, or the fore part of it, the latter part being devoted to

cleaning up and putting things in order.... December 25, 1846:
This day we have kept in the most solemn and sacred manner.
Our food for our Bodies has been bread and pure water, and the
food for our Souls has been to cleanse our hearts from all that's
wrong by means of confession. A day which every good believer
feels unspeakably thankful for.... January 1, 1847: We hailed
the new year this morning with two beautiful new songs at the
breakfast table, and marched one up to our rooms. And we
all wished each other with one united voice a happy and
comfortable new year, while we stood by our breakfast table.
I have seldom felt the prospects so cheering for a happy and
prosperous year.

A COMPLEX AND CHANGING STORY

It's convenient but incomplete to generalize about the Shakers as if they
were a homogeneous and static group. The full story is much more
complex. The Shaker movement lasted more than two centuries and
included nearly 17,000 people in several states. Of course, many changes
occurred over that period of time, and there were many variations from
one society to another. Other books tell the larger history. This book
gives just a slice of the story: I focus on the gardening practices and
the plants grown and sold in the nineteenth century when the Shaker
vegetable seed and medicinal herb businesses were at their peak, and
most of my examples are from the Shaker headquarters at New
Lebanon, New York.

It's also convenient but incomplete to talk about the Shakers in
the past tense. For many reasons, the Shaker movement gradually lost its
momentum and appeal. When Philemon Stewart hailed the New Year
in 1847, the society had reached its peak of about 6,000 members.
Membership dropped to fewer than 1,000 by 1900, fewer than 50
Believers remained in 1950, and in 1965 the remaining Shakers voted
to close the covenant of membership. Today seven Shakers still live at
Sabbathday Lake, Maine, and they grow and sell herbs. But their story
is the subject of a few other books, so I won't repeat it here.

THE SHAKER APPROACH
TO GARDENING

If you would have a lovely garden,
you should live a lovely life.
—SHAKER SAYING

AGRICULTURE AND HORTICULTURE were of primary importance to the
Shakers, who grew a wide variety of crops for their own use and for sale.
They planted hay, wheat, barley, oats, rye, and corn for their livestock;
raised potatoes, corn, squash, pumpkins, onions, beets, turnips, carrots,
asparagus, rhubarb, melons, strawberries, and other staples and luxuries
for the kitchen; tended orchards of apple, pear, peach, and cherry trees;
grew flax for fiber and broomcorn for brooms; and grew a large variety
of medicinal herbs. The Shakers could find a market for any of these
items if they had a surplus and often sold small amounts of this or that
to their neighbors. But for their major source of income, most Shaker
societies specialized in just one or a few garden products to grow in large
quantities. This combination of growing a wide diversity of crops for
their own use and a limited number of special crops to sell was typical
of early nineteenth-century farming. Like most farmers of their time,
the Shakers tried to supply as many of their own needs as possible, then
used income from their cash crops to buy whatever they couldn't grow
or make themselves. For most of the century, they were successful in all
regards: they ate well, lived comfortably, and had money left over.

The Shakers' success was due partly to their gardening
techniques, but mostly to their attitudes and values. Their devotion to
quality, their attention to detail, and their disciplined work habits
distinguished them from other farmers who were growing similar crops
and using similar techniques. For the Shakers, gardening was a spiritual
exercise, a way of putting belief into practice and taking responsibility

for creating a heaven on earth. The Shaker approach to gardening, like most aspects of Shakerism, was both practical and philosophical. As Elder Frederick Evans said, "Shakerism combines science, religion, and inspiration. It is a practical religion."

Although they didn't codify their approach to gardening under the exact headings I use below, my headings summarize and organize ideas that the Shakers expressed repeatedly in their sayings, journals, and publications. Work faithfully. Don't rush. Be attentive. Know your plants. Keep learning. Nurture the soil. Take care of your tools. Ideas like these are just as relevant today as they were 150 years ago.

AIM FOR PERFECTION; ACHIEVE IT
THROUGH DISCIPLINE AND HARD WORK

The Shakers didn't yearn for a ready-made garden of Eden where their needs would be effortlessly met. They were willing and eager to create their own paradise. They gladly undertook the task of transforming rough, formerly wooded sites into smooth, fertile, abundantly productive fields and gardens. This was a way of expressing their dedication, of doing God's work.

The Shaker vision of perfection was not just an aesthetic ideal, although they did have clear ideas about how a garden should look. Along with appearance, they emphasized performance, striving to "encourage onward"—that's a Shaker term—the quantity and quality of their harvests. As Marguerite Melcher wrote in *The Shaker Adventure*, "Men and women who had turned their eyes toward the goal of spiritual perfection could do no less than their best in the physical and material tasks that lay before them on earth.... If the earth could be made to produce larger crops, and if the quality of the plants grown could be improved from year to year, theirs was the responsibility for this improvement and this increase."

Especially in the early years, the Shakers were active proselytizers. They published many pamphlets explaining their beliefs and urging others to follow their ways. *The Gardener's Manual* shows how this fervor applied to gardening. This booklet, published by the Shakers at New Lebanon, was written by Charles Crosman in 1835, revised by Franklin Barber in 1843, and reissued several times over the next two decades. Priced at six cents, it was designed as a promotional tool to help

17

home gardeners succeed at growing vegetables so they would want to buy more Shaker seeds. The booklet is filled with solid practical advice, but its character comes from its Shakerly conviction and sense of mission. As the introduction states:

> The present condition of the majority of gardens in this country is susceptible of much improvement, which the spirit of the age, and the progressive improvements in agriculture, loudly demand. Many are unfavorably situated, and not large enough; many are of ill shape, and not well laid out internally. Very many are deficient in the variety of vegetables cultivated; and a majority not properly prepared before stocking with seeds and plants, and but poorly cultivated when stocked. These things should not be; the garden is said to be an index of the owner's mind. If this be true, many who otherwise might be acquitted, must be judged to possess minds susceptible of much improvement in order, usefulness, and beauty.

That one statement—"The garden is…an index of the owner's mind"—epitomizes the Shaker approach to gardening. It's a provocative remark, calculated to motivate self-appraisal. *The Gardener's Manual* exhorted readers to improve their minds as well as their gardens, recommending that gardening itself can provide a means for character development. For example, it points out that the management of a hotbed "is quite particular, and requires you to be thoughtful and regular; but this is only promoting a good habit, and if you were inclined to forgetfulness, would almost justify keeping one expressly for that purpose."

The Shakers were thoughtful and regular, and they worked hard. All residents, including children as young as three or four and elders in their seventies and eighties, regularly did some form of manual labor. In the fields and gardens, most of the planting and cultivating was done by a designated crew of brethren and boys; this crew typically numbered about one gardener per acre. The sisters and girls did most of the picking and processing of vegetables and fruits for the Shakers' own use and helped with picking, processing, and packaging the vegetable seeds, herbs, and other products that were sold. Throughout the year, workers moved from one task to another as needed. At the peak of harvest, though, everyone—men and women, young and old—worked together. Journal entries note these group efforts:

"October 16, 1850. We had a general bee this evening both Brethren & Sisters picking over beans for sale." "October 28, 1851. The Sisters making apple butter. They sit up till 3 o clock in the morning. Several Brethren assisted them. Made 3 barrels." "October 17, 1823. All hands turn out at digging potatoes and dig about 300 bushels."

KEEP THE GARDEN NEAT AND TIDY; MAKE THE ROWS STRAIGHT AND THE BEDS SQUARE

Open any gardening magazine today and you'll see gardens praised in phrases like "a glorious riot of color" or "a jumble of carefree perennials," where plants are allowed to "pop up," to "spill over," or to "intermingle" as they choose. To say the least, the Shakers would have seen no beauty in a riot, jumble, or jungle of unruly plants. They would have regarded such chaos as evidence of a lazy, careless gardener. They had a strict sense of regularity and order, and they kept their plants under control.

The directions were clear. Shaker gardens were neat squares or rectangles, because the Millennial Laws specified that "all walks must be laid straight, fields laid out square and fences built straight." Within a garden the rows were parallel and straight, plants were lined out at regular spacing, and runners and stalks were firmly tied to erect stakes, because "Zion is called to be a pattern of economy and order in all things." Weeds and litter were forbidden: "No kind of filthy rubbish may be left to remain around the dwelling houses or shops, nor in the door-yards or streets" and "No one should carelessly pass over small things, as a pin, a kernel of grain, etc. thinking it too small to pick up, for if we do, our Heavenly Father will consider us too small for him to bestow his blessing upon." And even the gardeners themselves had to be tidy: "No one should wear very ragged clothes, even about their work, if it can consistently be avoided."

The resulting neatness brought much satisfaction to the Shakers and also appealed to their visitors. As Benjamin Silliman, a traveler who passed through New Lebanon in 1819, wrote, "The utmost neatness is conspicuous in their fields, gardens, court yards, out houses, and in the very road; not a weed, not a spot of filth, or any nuisance is suffered to exist.... Such neatness and order I have not seen any where, on so large a scale, except in Holland."

19

WEED CEASELESSLY BY CULTIVATING, BUT DON'T USE MULCH

Judging from the journal entries, Shaker gardeners spent countless hours hoeing out weeds. Day after day is summed up in brief entries like "Hoeing," "Weeding and hoeing," "We hoe again," "We hoe most of the time," or this classic entry: "With the gardners it is weed weed hoe hoe because the weeds grow very fast."

The Gardener's Manual stated that "weeding should be early performed, and continued with persevering faithfulness, as often as necessary, through the season," and Shakers were advised, "Say not to thy friend, there are weeds in your garden, when thy own is choked with the same; but rather look at home." The emphasis on weeding goes beyond the requirements of horticulture; after all, vegetables can tolerate a few weeds without a serious reduction in yield. One explanation for this emphasis is that the Shakers compared cultivating a garden to cultivating the mind, and regarded weeding as a metaphor for spiritual cleansing. Pulling out weeds was like casting out impure thoughts. In that sense, the act of weeding was as beneficial for the gardener as it was for the garden.

Modern gardeners often control weeds by mulching rather than hoeing or pulling. Using mulch is efficient and effective, but the Shakers avoided it for various reasons. With so many livestock to feed and bed, they couldn't afford to use good hay and straw for mulch, especially for several acres at a time. They surely recognized that mulch can harbor rodents, insects, and plant diseases and that it sometimes brings weed seeds into a garden rather than preventing weeds. But most of all, with their concern for tidiness, it seems likely that the Shakers regarded mulch as unclean litter that defiled the purity of bare soil. The Shakers were fastidious about sweeping the floors of their buildings, and no less careful about their workshops, stables, and grounds. Mulch had no place in a society where cleanliness was next to godliness.

The few journal entries that do refer to mulch imply that it was used only to protect plants in winter. Elisha Myrick, who tended the herb garden at Harvard, Massachusetts, mentioned mulching in fall: on September 30, 1850, he wrote, "Cast the heap of waste stalks back of the herb house to the rose bushes in the east garden for mulching." Dead herb stalks make a good winter mulch for roses, sage, and other shrubs and perennials, because they're stiff and coarse enough to not compress into a sodden mass under the weight of the snow. But any winter mulches would have been removed in spring and added to the compost pile.

Early Shakers were probably familiar with Samuel Deane's *The New England Farmer, or Georgical Dictionary,* a book first published in 1797, reprinted many times, and widely read in its day. Many Shaker ideas and practices reflect Deane's thinking. For example, Deane defined mulch as "rubbish of decayed vegetables; litter is a word of the same import."

Several other entries in Deane's book have to do with the relationship between plants and air. In that era scientists were just beginning to learn about (but still didn't have names for) photosynthesis, respiration, oxygen, and carbon dioxide. Deane tried to piece together an understanding of these processes and concluded that it is very important for gardeners to provide plenty of air for their plants by cultivating the soil to loosen it around the roots and by spacing plants far enough apart that air can flow freely around the leaves. As he explained, "Effluvium [is] an invisible vapour consisting of minute particles, which exhales from bodies of almost every kind. A copious effluvium arises from all plants while they are growing; but more while drying after they are cut down, as appears from the strong and agreeable scent of mown grass." Live and dead animals, manure and compost, earth and water, and people also released effluvia, with the result that "the air is always so loaded with heterogeneous particles, that it is…considered by some as a kind of chaos. The air therefore contains much of the food of plants.… The fertilizing particles in the air easily enter the soil, when it is loose and open, and much exposed to the air." The idea of plants being nourished by invisible forces appealed to the spiritually oriented Shakers, so they hoed, as directed by *The Gardener's Manual,* "as often as necessary, for destroying weeds or *nourishing* [my emphasis] the plants through the season."

Like Deane, the Shakers faced the paradox that air *is* a kind of chaos, full of invisible particles both good and bad. The Shakers were notable in their concern for the quality of indoor air; they made unusual efforts to ventilate their buildings, convinced that "bad air" was a source of illness and that fresh air was essential for good health. Deane expressed this thinking with regard to plants: "A practical inference from

21

the copious perspiration of plants may be, that the plants we cultivate should not be set too close, that they may not be incommoded, or rendered sickly, by the unwholesome steams of each other." Reducing the amount of "unwholesome steam" in the garden is another reason for weeding. Summer days are steamy enough in the humid climates where the Shakers lived and gardened, and plants surrounded by damp stagnant air are more likely to be infected by blights, mildews, leaf spots, and other fungal diseases. Good ventilation is as important for plants as it is for people, and the Shakers' commitment to removing weeds so fresh air could flow between the plants helped keep their crops healthy. Also they thinned their crops to a generously wide spacing because, as *The Gardener's Manual* warned, "Leaving plants too thick is a prevalent error, and one to which gardeners are very liable."

USE THE MOST EFFICIENT TOOLS,
AND CARE FOR THEM PROPERLY

Growing vegetables and herbs requires but a few simple tools. *The Gardener's Manual* recommended that home gardeners could get by with "a plough, harrow, rake, hoes, spade, shovel, dung-fork, watering pot, transplanting-trowel, a long and strong line, or cord, and a wooden roller 18 inches in diameter and 4 feet long, [plus] bean poles, pea brush, a quantity of garden stakes and twine." The Shakers used these tools to grow their crops, and as with everything else, they kept the tools in good repair and stored them in an orderly manner.
The Millennial Laws directed: "All implements of labor, carts, waggons, sleighs, sleds, etc. should be put in their proper places on Saturday night, and as far as consistent every night. No one should take tools, belonging in charge of others, without obtaining liberty for the same. When any one borrows a tool, it should be immediately returned, without injury, if possible, and if injured, should be made known by the borrower to the lender."

It's worth noting that draft animals—an essential part of the garden work force—also received respectful care. The Millennial Laws directed that "no beasts belonging to the people of God may be left to suffer with hunger, thirst or cold, in consequence of neglect on the part of those who have the care of them. All should be kept in their proper places, and properly attended to according to their needs." Shakers were reminded that "no living thing may be chastened or corrected in a passion."

Now that old tools have become collector's items, as have all Shaker artifacts, it's tempting to romanticize the Shakers and their simple life, but this kind of imagining is often quite inaccurate, because it overlooks the scale on which they worked. At the peak of their enterprise, the Shaker gardeners were tending dozens of acres, harvesting hundreds of bushels of produce for their own kitchen, picking and packaging tons of herbs, and filling hundreds of thousands of seed packets. Doing all that work with simple hand tools was tedious and exhausting, so the Shakers were always looking for ways to be more efficient and productive.

This aspect of Shakerism is often misunderstood. Unlike the Amish, who cling to their old ways of working, the Shakers welcomed progress and technology. They readily accepted new tools and ideas and introduced many inventions themselves. Throughout the nineteenth century, they pursued horse-powered, water-powered, and steam-powered alternatives to traditional hand labor, especially for their large-scale operations. They were constantly inventing, testing, and revising equipment such as printing presses for printing seed packets, presses for packing their dried herbs into compact blocks, stills for distilling herb extracts, mowing machines, hay rakes, threshers, and other implements. Later, when electricity, tractors, automobiles, radios, and telephones became available, Shaker communities were often the first in their regions to acquire these conveniences, too.

While the processing of seeds and herbs was facilitated by new inventions, much of the outdoor garden work—sowing, transplanting, staking and tying stems, picking and sorting the harvest—remained as hand labor. The increased efficiency of processing put pressure on the gardeners to expand production. As often happens, adopting "labor-saving" devices did not mean the Shakers could relax and not work so hard. They were able to accomplish more, but they kept working as hard as ever, with the added responsibility that the machines themselves— generally prototypes or one-of-a-kind models designed especially by or for the Shakers—required frequent attention.

Within a department such as the vegetable seed or the medicinal herb industry, a single team of workers did everything from start to finish, from sowing seeds to filling orders. So the gardeners had to be their own mechanics, and they spent many rainy or wintery days fussing with machinery. Franklin Barber at New Lebanon expressed a positive but dutiful attitude toward machines—he really preferred being outdoors and working with plants. He wrote in his journal: "February 6, 1841. Repairing the machinery & making a new one for the purpose of shaking our great ridle [riddle—a sieve for sifting seeds] after altering making braking & having a great deal of trouble we finally succede & our machine works well & we think if carefully used will prove to be a great improvement and save much hard labour."

Other Shaker gardeners embraced mechanization. At Harvard, Elisha Myrick and George Allen worked for years to develop a horse-powered herb press, recovering bravely from innumerable setbacks. When they finally succeeded, Elisha was jubilant, writing in his journal: "December 31, 1854. We hail with delight every improvement relieving human toil or facilitating labor thus giving time and opportunity for moral, mechanical, scientific and intellectual improvement and the cultivation of the finer and higher qualities of the human mind."

NURTURE THE SOIL AND FERTILIZE IT GENEROUSLY

All too often, early American farmers treated soil as a resource to be mined. They made no effort to prevent erosion or to restore or replace the nutrients carried off the field when crops were harvested; instead, they abandoned old farms and moved farther west to start again with virgin land.

By contrast, the Shakers "looked upon the soil as something to be redeemed from rugged barrenness into smiling fertility and beauty." Although they did establish societies on promising sites in Ohio, Indiana, and Kentucky, most of the Shakers lived in eastern New York and New England, where the shallow, rocky soil definitely needs redemption. Committed to making the best of their situation, rather than moving away from it, the gardeners set to work. *The Gardener's Manual* outlined the task: "Deep, dry, light, and rich, are the essential requisites of a good garden soil; and if not so naturally, it should be made so. If wet, draining should be resorted to; if too shallow, deep ploughing; if poor, manuring; if stony, they should be got off:—and thus should every impediment and obstruction to a good sweet soil, be reversed or removed, by industry and art." The garden journals report the ongoing work of digging out stones, filling the holes, grading the fields to make them smooth and level, and, most important, applying cartloads of horse, cow, hog, and chicken dung and "vegetable manure" or compost.

The Gardener's Manual exhorted: "Here let it be stated, once for all, that all culinary vegetables do best upon a good rich soil; therefore let your land, if not naturally quite rich, be plentifully manured; and even if the land be quite fertile, if it has been used much, a slight manuring will be beneficial." Shaker fields were manured at least once a year, and the herb gardens were fertilized as heavily as the vegetable plots. The Shakers were unusually conscientious about maintaining soil fertility, compared to other farmers of their place and time.

Composting has been promoted so much in recent years that gardeners might be excused for thinking it's a new idea. In fact, it dates back at least two hundred years. Samuel Deane recommended composting in 1797 in *The New England Farmer.*

> Compost, a mixture of various manures and soils, to be laid on land to promote vegetation. Composts ought to be different, according to the different soils on which they are to be laid. A soil that is light and loose requires a compost that is heavy, or one which has a large proportion of the mud of deep ditches, swamps, or ponds, and cow-dung. But clayey and heavy lands require a compost in which something that is light and warm predominates, such as lime, the dung of horses and sheep, &c. Composts may be made of common earth, turfs, the dirt of streets, straw, mud, together with dung, lime, marle, ashes, weeds, salt, or oily substances, and any kind of animal or vegetable matters. They should be well mixed, and lie one year, one summer at least, in heaps, and be several times shoveled over to promote fermentation and putrefaction. They should be kept, if practicable, in a temperate degree of moisture.

Few farmers followed Deane's advice as conscientiously as the Shakers did. Maybe the Shakers found religious satisfaction in the way composting "redeems" trash and litter into valuable nutrients, or maybe they just appreciated composting as an efficient disposal system and an economical way to fertilize. At any rate, they regularly prepared compost from dead stalks and other garden debris, which they mixed with stable manure. Some individual Shaker gardeners were particularly avid composters, who devoted much attention to refining their recipes and methods and also experimented with lime, gypsum (often called plaster or plaster of Paris), wood ashes, guano, peat, seaweed, fish waste, pond mud, ground bones, and other fertilizers and soil amendments.

CONDUCT EXPERIMENTS, BE OBSERVANT, AND GIVE EACH PLANT THE CARE IT NEEDS

As entrepreneurs in the seed and herb business, the Shakers had to do their own research and development. There were no experts to consult and few books or publications to refer to. Fortunately, Shakerism encouraged curiosity, and the gardeners were free to conduct experiments and find their own answers to questions about how best to grow particular crops. Of course, some gardeners responded to the challenge more eagerly than others. Few were as deliberate as Franklin Barber at New Lebanon, who wrote journal entries like these: "Dunged one row of celery with rotten horse dung, another with rotted vegetable manure. Result: Vegetable appears best." "Beans, if planted before the ground gets warm are exposed to rot. I planted 7 beans May 8 and not one came up. Planted 10 beans July 8 from the same bag and 9 grew." "May 20, 1843. Sowed an experiment bed of seeds of all kinds, of the growth of 1838, to see which will germinate."

Barber was an observant gardener challenged by a very short growing season, and he was especially careful to notice how different vegetables were affected by spring and fall frosts. For example, he wrote that "corn in the spring will grow as long as the chit [terminal bud] is alive, and it requires very hard frosts to kill it. And this may be considered as a general rule for peppers and beans, but not for cucumber, squash etc. Tomatoes will grow after the chit is killed, sprouting out in new places."

Such careful attention to individual plants was typical of the

Shaker gardeners, and a key to their success. Hepworth Dixon, an Englishman who visited New Lebanon, described this approach:

> This morning I have spent an hour with [Elder Frederick Evans] in the new orchard, listening to the story of how he planted it....."A tree has its wants and wishes," said the Elder, "and a man should study it as a teacher watches a child, to see what he can do. If you love the plant, and take heed of what it likes, you will be well repaid by it. I don't know if a tree ever comes to know you; and I think it may; but I am sure it feels when you care for it and tend it, as a child does, as a woman does. Now, when we planted this orchard, we first got the very best cuttings in our reach; we then built a house for every plant to live in, that is to say, we dug a deep hole for each; we drained it well; we laid down tiles and rubble, and then filled in a bed of suitable manure and mould; we put the plant into its nest gently, and pressed up the earth about it; and protected the infant tree by this metal fence." "You take a world of pains," I said. "Ah, Brother Hepworth," he rejoined, "thee sees we love our garden."

DO EACH TASK IN ITS PROPER SEASON
AND KEEP WRITTEN RECORDS

The Shakers didn't make a habit of quoting from the Bible (they relied more on the words of their own early leaders, especially on the sayings of Mother Ann) but they surely were familiar with the famous passage in Ecclesiastes that begins, "For every thing there is a season.... A time to plant and a time to pluck up that which is planted."

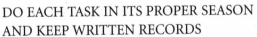

Shaker gardeners followed a well-worn path through the seasons, repeating the annual cycle of planting, tending, and harvesting their crops. Most of their work was so predictable that the timing of any particular event varied from year to year by just a few days or weeks, depending on the weather. Journal entries recorded this regularity: "June 9, 1820. The farmers go weading corn." "June 8, 1821. The farmers begin to hoe corn." "June 11, 1822. We hoe the corn." "June 13, 1823. We hoe the corn the first time."

Every gardener who's ever tried keeping a journal knows that it's very hard to write in it regularly but remarkably worthwhile if you do persevere. Most would-be journalists start with good intentions in spring, then lapse in the rush of summer, perhaps never to start again. The Shakers, with their disciplined habits, did better than average gardeners, often continuing year after year with several entries a week. Mixed in with the majority of the entries, which tell who did what work to which crop and what the weather was like, are notes on the flowering of fruit trees, the ripening of favorite vegetables such as tomatoes and cucumbers, and the arrival of robins and chirping of peeper frogs in spring.

Recording this kind of information over a period of time gives a gardener a reassuring sense of order, a sense that things happen when they *should* happen. Among the Shakers, most work was done so close to schedule that the gardeners seemed compelled to annotate any unusually early or late dates: "April 26, 1841. First plowing in the garden this year! late! late! late!!!!" "May 20, 1842. Today we sow the early cabbage. It is earlier than they are usually sown, but if they come to maturity too soon we can pull them up and put them in the cellar a little before the usual time, easier than we can make heads on them if they are sown too late."

One practice the Shakers may have followed, which is implied but not explicit in their writings, is phenology. This study uses the timing of annual occurrences such as bird migration or the leafing and flowering of hardy trees and shrubs as an indirect measure of temperature. Gardeners can use phenology to determine the best time for sowing seeds, as expressed in the old saying that it's safe to plant corn when the oak leaves are the size of a squirrel's ear. This system works. By the time the soil is warm enough for oak leaves to expand, it's warm enough for corn seeds to germinate and not rot, and any subsequent frosts will be too mild to damage the germinating shoots. With a little deliberate experimenting and several years of records, an observant gardener can identify phenological markers for many seasonal tasks. Samuel Deane recommended this approach in *The New England Farmer* (he attributed the idea to Linnaeus, but it may be even older than that), and it's likely that at least some of the Shaker gardeners put the idea into practice.

KNOW PLANTS BY NAME

Many gardeners grow excellent plants without knowing their Latin names or even their common names—naming isn't a necessary part of gardening. The Shakers could have filled their kitchens, pantries, and root cellars without worrying about names. But they couldn't treat their cash crops that way. In selling vegetable seeds and medicinal herbs, they had to be very careful to correctly identify and name their plants.

Not everyone who worked in the gardens would have been expected to know all the plants. That was the responsibility of the head gardeners, who took the role seriously. Unlike most Shaker products, such as brooms, furniture, textiles, and other handcrafted or manufactured goods, which were typically unsigned, Shaker seeds and herbs were associated with particular brethren, whose names were listed prominently on the catalogs. These men epitomized the Shaker reputation for quality, and the societies depended on their knowledge and integrity.

In the case of vegetable seeds, the Shakers used variety names, such as Early Canada corn, Cranberry bean, or Black Winter radish. The head of the seed garden needed to know what distinguished each variety, so he could tell which was which and keep them separate, a task that grew more complicated as the number of varieties increased. In the 1850s, under the direction of master seedsman Jefferson White, the Enfield, Connecticut, society was offering twenty-two kinds of beans, nine kinds of beets, sixteen of cabbages, nineteen of cantaloupes and watermelons, eleven of lettuce, twelve of peas, nine of squash, and fourteen of turnips, as well as fewer types of many other vegetables. (Imagine being able to distinguish among fourteen kinds of turnips!)

Because the seed growers knew how each variety was supposed to turn out, they could monitor the developing crops and cull individual plants that were atypical or not "true to type." This culling was essential to maintain the standards for that variety. They also watched for individual plants that rose above average; sometimes these were propagated and introduced as new varieties, such as the "Great Austin Shaker Seedling Strawberry, the Largest Strawberry in the World," with "berries measuring five inches," and "as remarkable for flavor as for size and thrift."

In addition, each seed grower had to compare what he was growing with the varieties offered by other Shakers and by their competitors in the World, to determine if everyone was using the same names for the same varieties. Sometimes they weren't; essentially identical plants might have two different names, or the same name might be used for different plants. For example, Franklin Barber noted in his journal that "it appears that Rose Radish and Salmon Radish are synonymous, or but one kind," and that "the Hancock gardeners call Summer Scallop Squash, Dutch Bush Squash." These situations were ambiguous, but the seedsmen did their best to reduce the confusion.

The brethren in charge of the herb departments had an even more difficult task than the vegetable seed growers. They had to know the Latin and common names for as many as 300 to 400 different kinds of herbs (not all were cultivated; many were collected from the woods and waysides). Several of these medicinal herbs are quite poisonous, so accurate identification is a life-or-death matter. The herbalists had to know the plants well enough to distinguish between very similar-looking species and to identify them correctly even when they were not in bloom, by recognizing the appearance, fragrance, or other characteristics of the foliage or roots.

The Shaker herbalists relied on the best available references for identifying and naming their plants and often cited these references in their catalogs. Catalogs from Canterbury, New Hampshire, in the 1830s stated, "The common names in this catalogue are such as are generally used in the New England states. The Botanical names are from Eaton's Manual of Botany, last editions." Amos Eaton's *Manual,* first published in 1817, was superseded in 1848 by Asa Gray's work, and most Shakers adopted the new reference, as noted in an 1860 catalog from Watervliet: "For the generic and specific names, we have relied on Gray's *Botany of the Northern United States*—adopting those common names best known among druggists, herbalists, and botanic physicians. Gray's, we believe, is now considered the standard." In the late 1800s, several of the herb catalogs addressed the babel of common names by including lists of synonyms. Reading the old catalogs, a modern herb gardener can recognize most of the Shaker herbs by their Latin names, but it's surprising how few of the old common names are still used today.

GROW USEFUL PLANTS, NOT MERE ORNAMENTALS

From the beginning, the Shakers planted field crops, vegetables, fruits, and herbs, but virtually no flowers or ornamental trees or shrubs. No doubt this was partly a practical matter—the gardeners were too busy with essential crops to bother with luxuries that couldn't be eaten or sold. Some of the seed catalogs did mention "flower seeds, assorted, put up in neat papers," but the garden journals don't record the planting and harvesting of flower seeds. Apparently the quantities were small; perhaps growing flower seeds was too small a job to mention, or perhaps the Shakers simply purchased flower seeds and packaged them for resale.

Besides being too busy, the gardeners did not grow ornamentals for another reason: they were discouraged from it by the early Shaker elders, as described by Sister Marcia Bullard in "Shaker Housekeeping," published in *Good Housekeeping* magazine in July 1906.

> Forty years ago it was contrary to the "orders" which governed our lives to cultivate useless flowers, but fortunately for those of us who loved them, there are many plants which are beautiful as well as useful.... The rose bushes were planted along the sides of the road which ran through our village and were greatly admired by the passerby, but it was strongly impressed upon us that a rose was useful, not ornamental. It was not intended to please us by its color or its odor, its mission was to be made into rose-water, and if we thought of it in any other way we were making an idol of it and thereby imperiling our souls.... In order that we might not be tempted to fasten a rose upon a dress or to put it into water to keep, the rule was that the flower should be plucked with no stem at all.

Actually, the Millennial Laws did not specifically forbid the growing of flowers, and different societies may have been more or less strictly opposed to them. One cryptic journal entry from 1843 had the New Lebanon gardeners spending a pleasant Saturday in May "enjoying the garden" and "fixing the flowers." Another from 1847 refers to fruit trees "by the Pink bed." That might mean clove pinks, *Dianthus caryophyllus.* Pinks were very popular in colonial New England, and they were included on a Shaker seed list from Hancock in the 1830s. But the Laws did state that "Believers may not spend their time cultivating fruits and plants, not adapted to the climate in which they live." Believers were not allowed to indulge in useless animals, either; the Laws specified that "no kinds of beasts, birds, fowls, or fishes, may be kept merely for the sake of show, or fancy" and that "no Believer is allowed to play with cats or dogs."

Modern gardeners who find these restrictions difficult to understand or accept will be relieved to learn that the Shakers eventually revised their policy on ornamental plants (they were slow to embrace pets, though). When the rules were relaxed after the Civil War, Shakers responded by planting flowers, shrubs, and trees around the dwelling houses and other buildings and by cutting bouquets to bring indoors. By the twentieth century, flower gardening was even recommended as a wholesome form of recreation for the girls and sisters. But by that time the Shakers were so diminished in numbers and influence that their flower-growing activities never gained a fraction of the attention given to their vegetables and herbs.

A basket of tansy is ready for drying.

*The Shaker communities typically owned hundreds of acres of land,
including woods, pastures, orchards, cultivated fields, and gardens.*

Apples were an important food in early America,
and the Shakers grew several varieties to eat fresh,
store for winter use, and make cider, applesauce, and pie.

In the late 1800s, the Shakers began to decorate their landscapes with flower beds and ornamental trees and shrubs.

Shaker buildings were designed to be sturdy, practical, convenient, and comfortable.

The Shakers valued neatness and order, and planted their vegetables in straight, parallel rows.

Most of the Shaker communities were dismantled decades ago,
but a few remain today and are open to visitors. This is
Hancock Shaker Village in Massachusetts.

Men and boys did most of the garden work,
such as hoeing and weeding.

By May the seedlings are ready to transplant into the garden.

OPPOSITE PAGE:
A hotbed is an ideal place to raise seedlings, starting in late winter.
A four-foot pile of composting horse manure provides heat from below,
and glass sashes on top protect the seedlings from cold, wind, and snow.

Vegetables like these onions thrive in fertile soil.
The Shakers applied plenty of compost to their
gardens every year.

OPPOSITE PAGE:
The Shakers invented the system of selling seeds
in small paper packets rather than in bulk.
They supplied merchants with wooden display boxes,
which they refilled with fresh seeds each year.

Corn was a staple crop for the Shakers. They used cornmeal
for baking and ate fresh and dried sweet corn.

PREVIOUS PAGES:
The technique of canning vegetables was invented in
the late 1840s, and the Shakers were quick to adopt it.

48

SHAKER IDEAS
FOR TODAY'S KITCHEN GARDEN

*We have therefore endeavored to furnish
a small and convenient Manual, which we trust
will prove beneficial to all who…have had but
little experience in cultivating a kitchen garden,
by furnishing such plain and practical directions
as are best calculated to ensure success.*
—INTRODUCTION TO THE GARDENER'S MANUAL

IT WASN'T ENOUGH for the Shakers just to tend their own gardens. To succeed in the seed business, they needed an audience of satisfied customers who would reorder year after year. But many Americans in the 1800s were unfamiliar with growing vegetables and didn't know how to plant or tend a garden, so the Shakers tried to expand their market by publishing *The Gardener's Manual; Containing Plain Instructions for the Selection, Preparation, and Management of a Kitchen Garden: With Practical Directions for the Cultivation and Management of Some of the Most Useful Culinary Vegetables.* I have already quoted from this pamphlet to illustrate the general Shaker approach to gardening. Here I'll discuss some of its practical advice.

CHOOSING A GARDEN SITE

The Gardener's Manual said, "In choosing a site for a garden, a spot of even land, slightly inclining to the south or east, and having the full benefit of the sun, is to be preferred. It should be situated near the dwelling, and neatly enclosed with a high wall, or a tight board fence."

This is excellent advice on all counts. A level or gently sloping site in full sun is ideal for growing vegetables. If a garden is convenient to the house, you'll tend it more faithfully. A wall or fence is expensive to build, but it shelters plants from cold winds and keeps out critters.

GARDEN SIZE

The Gardener's Manual said, "The size of a garden depends upon the number to be supplied from it, and the kinds of vegetables intended to be raised in it. For a family of six persons, one quarter of an acre is sufficient for most of the kinds raised from seeds commonly retailed at the country stores. But if desirable to have fruit trees, shrubs, strawberry beds, early potatoes, &c., enclosed within the same fence that encloses the garden, it must be made larger, in proportion to the quantity wanted."

The Gardener's Manual was intended for farm families that had plenty of land, livestock to provide draft power and manure, and several children to help hoe and weed. Even so, I'm surprised that the Shakers would encourage novice vegetable growers to plant a quarter-acre plot. The most common problem among new gardeners is starting with too big an area, then getting discouraged by the chore of maintaining it all and overwhelmed by the magnitude of the harvest.

Here's an interesting comparison. In 1843 the Shakers recommended planting a quarter acre, or 11,000 square feet; that would be almost 2,000 square feet apiece for a six-person family. A century later, in World War II, the Victory Garden Committee recommended planting 1,000 square feet of garden area for each person in the family, noting that "a family of five would have a garden 50 by 100 or 5,000 square feet—which would keep one person rather busy during spare time." Families today plant even smaller vegetable gardens, often less than 1,000 square feet in total, and feel rushed to keep up with that. Gardens have shrunk because we have less land and less spare time, and because we tend to plant less of the bulky subsistence crops such as potatoes and dry beans and more of the smaller, gourmet plants such as fancy salad greens.

A RECIPE FOR COMPOST

The Gardener's Manual advised, "The best manure for a garden is a compost, of one part mineral substances, as ashes, lime, sand or clay, (as the soil may require,) salt, &c.: five parts vegetable matter, as weeds, straw, leaves, roots and stalks of plants, and tan bark or sawdust to make the soil light, if necessary: and six parts of animal excrement. These should be collected in the course of the season, and mixed well together, to cause them to ferment. In the fall, this compost should be spread evenly upon the garden, and ploughed in."

Most gardeners today make compost rather haphazardly as a way to dispose of clippings, stalks, garden debris, and kitchen waste. The Shakers were more deliberate about measuring the ingredients and maintaining the ratios of mineral, plant, and animal matter. Gardeners at Hancock Shaker Village in Massachusetts who have followed this recipe say that it works very well—the compost heats up readily and transforms into a crumbly "black gold." The parts should be measured by volume, such as a bushel basket, garden-cart load, or pickup-truck load. It's worth the effort of mixing or turning the pile at least twice as it ferments, because that makes the ingredients decompose more quickly and completely.

The Gardener's Manual recommended applying compost at a rate of up to forty ox-cart loads per acre. How much is an ox-cart load? I'm not sure, but let's say it's about one cubic yard. If so, forty loads is the equivalent of a three-inch layer of compost spread over the entire garden. That's the rate for poor land; "on good land, less will suffice." Gardeners today use comparable amounts of compost if they can keep up with the process of making it and have enough of the raw ingredients.

The Shakers recommended spreading the compost on the garden in the fall and working it into the soil, not leaving it on the surface. This was partly an expression of their passion for neatness, but it was also an adaptation to the climate in New Lebanon, where the typical spring is cool and wet, with a chance of snow as late as May. Tilling in fall and leaving a garden uncovered makes the soil dry out faster so you can start planting earlier in spring. Fall tilling also helps eliminate insects and diseases that overwinter in the soil.

PREPARING RAISED BEDS FOR PLANTING
The Gardener's Manual listed several steps in preparing the soil. (This was for an existing garden; breaking new ground added even more steps.) After spreading the compost, first comes plowing, and "deep ploughing is the only kind wanted in preparing a garden, the deeper the better in most soils." Actually, a horse-drawn plow inverts only the top six to eight inches of soil. In small gardens you can dig at least that deep

51

with a spade or fork.

"Next comes the harrow; this should do its work faithfully." The purpose of harrowing is to break up clods, which you can do by thumping with the tines of a digging fork. After a few years of adding compost to the soil, you won't have many clods.

Then comes "a second and last ploughing, dividing the garden into beds." This is done by plowing around and around each bed, turning the earth from both sides toward the center. "This plan of ploughing and forming beds, will leave little hollows or ditches between them, which should be kept open to drain off the superabundant water in wet weather." You can do the same thing with a hoe, mounding the soil into beds that are raised a few inches and are as wide and long as you choose.

"The next thing is to rake the beds; which, on those designed for fine seeds or those to be sown in drills [rows], should be thoroughly and finely done. On those designed for planting beans, squashes, &c., you need not be so particular." Nor do you have to be so particular about raking beds designed for tomatoes, peppers, and other crops that are transplanted rather than sown in place.

The Gardener's Manual noted that "some gardeners sow and plant many kinds of seeds upon ridges. For some seeds, especially in low flat land, this is a good practice." Ridges are narrow raised beds made by throwing two plow furrows together and raking to level the top. For seeds such as corn, squash, and pole beans, "make hills, or slight elevations of the soil, a foot in diameter and three inches high, with a southern inclination." (That means the top of the hill should slant toward the south, so the sun can warm and dry the soil.)

Planting on raised beds, ridges, or hills is an excellent practice in cool, damp climates or where the soil is wet and heavy. In warm, dry climates or sandy soil, it's usually better to plant at ground level, because raised plantings dry out too fast and require extra watering.

SOWING SEEDS IN ROWS AND HILLS
The Gardener's Manual said, "Stretch a line from end to end, over your bed, for a guide in drilling, then with the corner of your hoe, a pointed stick, or an instrument made for the purpose, drill shallow furrows across the bed from north to south, in depth and distance apart,

accommodated to the kinds of seeds you wish to sow." That's for sowing seeds in rows. For sowing in hills, "Stretch the line as directed for sowing, but instead of drilling make hills." In either case "the earth should always be pressed upon the tops of the seeds. On level beds, it may be done with a roller; on seeds planted in hills, with the back of the hoe."

Shaker gardeners did repeated experiments on the effects of soaking seeds before sowing them, with inconclusive results. According to *The Gardener's Manual*, "In a very dry season, or when you happen to be very late in stocking your garden, soaking the seed a few hours, in luke-warm water, will be beneficial to some kinds; but generally, if sown in proper season, all good seeds will germinate quite as well without soaking, and to seeds of the cabbage kind, it is a positive injury."

Entries for particular crops, in the second half of *The Gardener's Manual*, told whether to plant the seeds early when the soil is still cool or after the soil is fully warm, and specified how far apart and how deep to sow the seeds, and how much to thin the seedlings. In general, "thinning may be performed twice, the first time as soon as the plants are fairly in sight, the second after they are large enough to show which will make thrifty plants. As the quality of the crop, as well as the quantity, frequently depends very much upon this branch of cultivation, it is important that it be seasonably and faithfully performed."

STARTING SEEDS IN A HOTBED

A hotbed is a pile of fermenting manure with a cold frame on top. Heat from the fermentation warms the soil in the cold frame, making it possible to grow tender plants even when the weather is chilly. Market gardeners in the Boston area began using hotbeds in the 1750s (as soon as glass sashes for making the cold frames were available and affordable) to produce early crops of lettuce and radishes for market, to force the ripening of strawberries and melons, and to raise seedlings. The Shakers used hotbeds primarily to grow seedlings. Making a hotbed is a big job, and maintaining it takes constant watchfulness, but the Shakers were so pleased with the potential of hotbeds for growing sturdy seedlings that they strongly urged home gardeners to try them. The gardeners today at Hancock Shaker Village make a hotbed each spring to raise seedlings for their demonstration garden, and their seedlings look much more vigorous and stocky than typical modern seedlings grown indoors in artificial soil and artificial light. The only drawback is that you need a big pile of fresh horse manure—that may be hard to find in your neighborhood!

I make a modern-style hotbed by laying an electric soil-heating cable in the bottom of my cold frame each spring. That's much easier and it works in virtually the same way. Whether you use manure or electricity to heat the hotbed, the information in *The Gardener's Manual* is so clear, accurate, and helpful that I'll give it here in full:

> Such vegetables as are wanted for early use, or such as require the whole season to bring them to maturity, may be brought forward nearly a month earlier, by being sown early in a hot-bed, and transplanted in the open ground, when the weather has become mild and the soil prepared for vegetation. The hot-bed should always be located on the south side of a building, or a high wall. The frame to receive the sashes should be four feet wide, and as long as you desire, the inclination to the south will be about right if the back of the frame is 18 inches high to have the front 9 inches. To this frame, let the sashes be nicely fitted, to exclude rats, mice, and cold weather.
>
> Having prepared the frame, find its dimensions, and mark out the spot for building the bed 6 inches larger every way, than the frame; drive down a stake at each corner as an aid in building the bed. For this, the best material is unfermented horse dung, with the litter or straw among it, as it usually comes from the stable. In taking from a heap of this, get the inside as well as the out, both long and short, and mix them well together. If the litter be not in the proportion of one half or more, increase it by adding fresh straw. Take this to the spot where you are to make your bed, put it on, a forkful at a time, shaking it well to pieces, spreading it evenly, and beating it well down as you proceed, particularly the edges. Raise it to the height of 4 feet, then put on the frame, and let it stand till the heat rises.
>
> Now put within the frame, on the top of the dung, 8 inches in depth, of light, rich soil, then cover it all up, and let it stand a week or more, till the earth is well warmed, when it may be sown. Make the drills from north to south, and 3 inches apart, in depth according to the kind of seeds sown.

Journal entries noted that the gardeners at New Lebanon usually prepared and planted their hotbeds in late March. And one entry added this advice: "The soil for a hot-bed should be very porous, that it may absorb the water readily, when you water it; mixing it with rotten horse dung finely pulverized, will promote this and hasten the growth of the plants besides. Common earth is apt to crust over and cause the water to run off instead of penetrating the soil. To further prevent this, the earth in a hot bed should be nearly level on the top."

Now back to *The Gardener's Manual.* Having sown the seeds,

From this time the bed must be watched and attended with particular care. Every morning, as soon as the sun is fairly up, the glasses should be raised a little, to admit fresh air; and in a warm day they may be entirely removed. If the glasses are left on, under a hot sun, without the admission of air, more than two hours, the plants will be scalded by the steam thus excited within the bed. More failures arise in hot-bed culture, from want of air, than from all other causes combined.

Watering is a very essential part of the hot-bed management; it should be done in the morning, with a fine sprinkler, and with water the temperature of rain in summer. The earth should often be mellowed among the plants, to admit the water freely, and promote their growth; weeds should be uprooted, and the suggestions concerning thinning should be most punctually attended to; as a rule, a plant in the hot-bed should be as distant from another plant, as its top or longest shoot is from its own root.

Many regard hot-beds as more expensive than profitable, but this is an error.... In a large garden a good hot-bed will more than pay for itself, annually, and in any garden, worthy of the name, the benefits are double the expense.

TRANSPLANTING SEEDLINGS

The Gardener's Manual said:

A prevalent, but erroneous opinion concerning transplanting is, that it should be done just before a shower, in order to succeed well; but experience has shown that a day or two after, when the

55

ground has become dry enough to work again, in the evening, is a preferable time, and perhaps, with the exception of cloudy weather, is the best that can be selected. The ground should be prepared as directed for sowing, the plants should be taken up with as much dirt as possible adhering to them, which will be promoted by watering plentifully, before taking them up. A hole deep enough for the roots to enter at full length, should be made, the plants set upright, and fine fresh earth gently pressed against the roots on all sides. Tender plants will sometimes need watering and shading a day or two after transplanting.

This is all excellent advice, but did you wonder why there's no warning about hardening off seedlings before transplanting them? That's because seedlings grown in a hotbed with sashes open in the daytime are already adapted to outdoor conditions. Only soft seedlings that have been grown indoors need the gradual transition called hardening off.

WATERING AND CULTIVATING
The Gardener's Manual observed:

Some gardeners spend much useless labor in sprinkling water over and around their plants. When the ground is very dry, at the time you wish to transplant, watering the ground where you intend to set the plants, a day or two beforehand, may be beneficial: watering hot beds is also necessary and indispensable. But to plants in open ground, that have good roots, watering in the customary way, with a hand watering pot, is of but little use. If you have a stream of running water at your command, which can be turned upon your garden, something more effectual may be performed. But in default of this, digging and stirring the soil should be resorted to, which will cause the moisture below the surface, the *life and dependance of plants in a dry time*, to rise freely.

Gardeners in the 1800s didn't have pumps, hoses, sprinklers, or any other irrigation equipment. If it didn't rain, all they could do was carry water in buckets, a few gallons at a time. One gallon—even one cup—of water can spell the difference between life and death to a little seedling or transplant, but a gallon is an insignificant quantity to a larger plant in the midst of a summer drought. Instead of sprinkling, *The Gardener's Manual* recommended cultivating. This advice may sound counterintuitive, for stirring the soil would seem to allow its moisture to evaporate into the air. But cultivating does encourage the capillary action that draws water up through the soil; moreover, it forms what's called a "dust mulch"—a surface layer, one or more inches deep, of dust-fine soil particles that actually serves as a barrier to evaporation. An old-fashioned dust mulch can retain soil moisture just as effectively as the organic mulches so popular today. Try it and see.

INSECT PEST CONTROL

The Gardener's Manual recommended nontoxic controls for some of the most common pests of vegetable gardens. These strategies are worth a try today.

Cutworms "prey upon Beans, Corn, Peppers, Onions, Radishes, and Cabbage plants, in their infant state, cutting off the leaves and sometimes the stems or stalks." To kill this insect, look "under the dirt, near the plant which it last destroyed; there it may be found and easily destroyed."

Root-worms or root maggots "attack the roots of all plants, of the cabbage kind, those of melons and cucumbers, and are well known to be especially fond of turnips and radishes. To prevent their depredation, pour old fermented urine, salt water, or weak lye, directly around the roots, or what is the same in effect, scatter around a little salt, or wood ashes. As a preventative, which is ever preferable to a cure, never put these vegetables on the same ground they occupied the previous year."

For slugs, strew "ashes or quick lime over them."

Cabbage-lice (aphids) "always infest the weakest, poorest plants." They can ruin a crop, so take action as soon as you detect a problem, "before the lice become so numerous as to render it an impracticable undertaking. Plaster, ashes, or quick lime, sprinkled over them in a dewy morning will check their progress; but will not destroy them, unless rubbed in. To effect this, a brush or cloth may be used, unfolding the leaves with one hand and applying the brush with the other. A decoction of tobacco, administered with a sponge in the same way, is very effectual; fermented urine is equally so."

The turnip-fly or garden-flea (flea beetle) is a tiny black insect which attacks plants in their infant state, feasting upon their tender leaves to the great annoyance of the gardener and destruction of the plants. Melons, cucumbers, squashes, cabbages, and turnips, are their favorite food. Covering the plants with chaff, fine shavings, or sawdust, till they are out of danger, we have found to be the most effectual mode of preventing their ravages. When this can not be afforded, snuff, soot, or sulphur finely pulverised, and sprinkled over and under the plants while wet with dew is beneficial. But as plants are subject to material injury from these insects, only while in an infant state, the chief aim should be to have the land so prepared, seeded, and cultivated, as to give the plants a vigorous, thrifty growth, which will soon place them out of danger.

Yellow or striped bugs (striped cucumber beetles) are "another enemy of the Cucumber tribe. Its depredations may be essentially checked by sprinkling the plants when wet, with a composition of Rye-flour, Ashes and Plaster, having equal quantities of each, thoroughly mixed. Water saturated with cow-dung, is also said to be a good remedy."

Finally, *The Gardener's Manual* recommended sowing extra seeds as insurance against crop loss, because "all means of preventing the ravages of insects may at times fail." Despite their best efforts, the Shakers themselves sometimes lost a crop to insects, as noted in these journal entries from New Lebanon: "June 26, 1847. The 3 aged brethren work destroying worms [caterpillars] upon the parsnips....The worms appear 10 times worse than ever, we have put tobacco juice, strong soap suds, Guano Juice, Salt and Lime on them, but it does not kill them or keep them off, therefore we have gone to squishing them with our fingers." "July 6, 1847. The Brethren and Sisters all turn out this and last evening after supper and go to killing worms upon the parsnips. Our seed by them is already literally destroyed."

SHAKER VEGETABLES
AND VEGETABLE SEEDS

The tomato is a very healthy vegetable, and
a great favorite when we become accustomed to it,
although generally not very palatable at first.
—THE GARDENER'S MANUAL

IN THE 1790S, soon after the Shakers established their first settlements in
Watervliet and New Lebanon, New York, they began selling seeds from
their vegetable gardens. The business grew quickly. By 1800 the society
at New Lebanon was already selling about $1,000 worth of onion, beet,
carrot, cucumber, summer squash, radish, turnip, cabbage, and other
vegetable seeds each year. One thousand dollars was a lot of money in
those days, and the other Shaker societies were so impressed by this
opportunity that they started their own seed businesses. The societies at
Enfield, Connecticut, and Union Village, Ohio, developed very large and
successful seed businesses, and several other villages sold smaller but still
valuable amounts of vegetable seeds.

A HISTORICAL VIEW OF THE
SHAKER VEGETABLE SEED BUSINESS
Selling $1,000 worth of seeds is not the same as making $1,000 profit,
but Isaac Youngs at New Lebanon, writing in 1836, estimated that "after
deducting the [dealer's] discount and loss in old seeds, etc.,...the Nett
income is about 1/2 of the retail price." For a small group of gardeners
working on stony land in a cold climate, the business of growing seeds
was unusually lucrative. What accounts for the Shakers' success?

For one thing, they spotted an opportunity where there wasn't
much competition in 1800. A few merchants in major cities such as
Boston, New York, and Philadelphia sold seeds imported from England,
but average gardeners in small towns or on the frontier could get seeds

only by saving their own from year to year or by trading with relatives and neighbors. Although the gardeners at Watervliet and New Lebanon were not quite the first people to grow and sell seeds in the United States—David Landreth had started a seed business in Pennsylvania a few years earlier, in 1784—the Shakers were among the first domestic suppliers, and that was to their advantage.

The Shakers sold some seeds directly to gardeners by peddling from door to door, but mostly they sold through dealers or general stores. In both cases, they gained an early advantage because of one significant innovation. The Shakers invented the idea of packaging seeds in small packets, or papers, as they called them. Previously, seeds had been packed in large cloth bags, barrels, or bins and sold in bulk. Shopkeepers didn't have room to keep many big bags or bins in their store, so variety was limited. By contrast, the Shakers provided a convenient display box that could fit right on the counter. Now a store could stock dozens of kinds of seeds in less space than was previously filled by a single bag or barrel. This appealed to the merchants and to the customers, too.

Putting seeds in small packets had many advantages. It encouraged gardeners to try new varieties and to expand their gardens. The packets were labeled, so customers could keep track of which seeds were which. And selling in smaller quantities helped the Shakers develop and maintain a reputation for quality. When seeds were sold in bulk and merchants bought large quantities, it wasn't uncommon for the seeds to go stale before they were sold. Gardeners then as now were disappointed when stale seeds failed to grow or produce well. The Shakers emphasized the freshness and vitality of their seeds, convinced that freshness was critical to the customer's success. (They also emphasized the purity of their seeds and took care to eliminate the weed seeds, chaff, and other debris that sometimes contaminated their competitors' seed packets.) The small packets made it easy for merchants to stock only as many seeds as they could expect to sell in a year. Further, the Shakers often allowed dealers to take seeds on consignment rather than buying them outright. Traveling Shaker salesmen made annual rounds, delivering boxes filled with an assortment of new seeds and retrieving the previous year's boxes. The merchant paid only for the seeds that had sold. Back at the Shaker workshops, the unsold seeds were sorted and repackaged or discarded, as appropriate.

Another reason for the Shakers' success was that they entered the vegetable seed business just as the market was starting to expand. In 1800 Americans ate more meat and bread and not as many vegetables as we do now. So at first the Shakers had to promote their product to an uninformed and unenthusiastic audience. They had to convince potential buyers that vegetables are good to eat and that tending a vegetable garden is worth the effort. But along with the Shakers, many other individuals and groups were telling Americans to eat more vegetables, and soon the national diet changed. By midcentury, people were eating much larger quantities of a much wider variety of vegetables. Meanwhile the market was growing because the country was growing. The population was increasing fast, the economy was strong, and many families had enough land to plant a garden.

But as the market expanded, so did the competition. By the 1820s and 1830s, neighboring Shaker villages were encroaching on each other's territories and cutting into each other's profits. By 1841 it was clear to the New Lebanon gardeners that "by reason of others as well as ourselves raising and selling so many seeds the market has become [flooded].... [It] appears to be almost useless to try to raise seeds expecting to sell them & get what they are worth....We are almost afraid we shall have to fling many of them away, for we have now upon hand I should think $10,000 worth."

Rivalry within the Society of Believers was strong, and competition between Shakers and non-Shakers was even more challenging. (Most distressing of all, perhaps, was competition between Shakers and ex-Shakers such as Charles F. Crosman, who wrote the first edition of *The Gardener's Manual* at New Lebanon in 1835 but left the Shakers a few years later to start his own seed company in Rochester.) By 1850 there were dozens of seed companies in New York and New England, so the market was saturated and prices were down. By now everyone was putting seeds in packets and coming up with other new schemes—putting lovely illustrations on the packets, issuing colorful mail-order catalogs, offering premiums. The Shakers adopted some of these practices, but they did so reluctantly. They weren't aggressive competitors. They wanted to succeed on the basis of quality, not style.

Most of the Shaker seed businesses reached their peak sales in the 1840s or 1850s and declined more or less swiftly afterward. The Shakers were already discouraged by competition when the Civil War disrupted sales, and they found it hard to recover. By the 1870s the Shakers could no longer recruit enough new members, especially young men, to keep up with the work of growing, packaging, and selling seeds. And as railroads crossed the country, not only the Shakers, but most farmers throughout the Northeast found they couldn't compete with the cheaper land, better soil, and milder climates of California and other western states. So in the 1890s, about one hundred years after their seed business began, the Shakers at New Lebanon closed it down. Most of the other Shaker societies had already closed theirs.

In sum, the Shakers had the advantage of getting an early start in an expanding market, and they invented a packaging system that was convenient, attractive, and popular with both merchants and customers. They earned an excellent reputation for the quality, purity, and freshness of their seeds. Eventually, though, the businesses were overwhelmed by competition and by changes inside and outside the Society of Believers.

A GARDENER'S VIEW OF THE SEED BUSINESS

The seed business may have been lucrative, at least for a time, but to judge from the gardeners' journals, growing and selling vegetable seeds was tedious, exhausting, and worrisome. The scale of the effort was daunting. For example, in the 1840s the Shakers at New Lebanon had three gardens devoted to vegetable seed production, with a total area of about five and a half acres. A crew of five men and boys, on average, did all the routine work in these gardens, with extra help only for especially big or urgent jobs. In spring and early summer, they prepared the soil, raised seedlings in hotbeds, planted all the crops, and started the endless tasks of weeding and hoeing. Throughout the summer and fall, they harvested cartloads of ripe seedpods and mature vegetables and separated out bushels of seeds. From late fall to early spring, they cleaned and sorted the seeds, then cut, folded, pasted, filled, sealed, labeled, boxed, and shipped more than 100,000 packets of seeds each year.

Typical journal entries tally the work: "August 2, 1841. Harvested 5 bushels of early pea seeds from 1/3 acre, worth $4 per bushel." "September 30, 1843. Got in the beets intended for seed next year as follows: 1700 bloods, 1500 white, 600 yellow, 600 turnip, 500 scarcity. Set out in cellar." "October 19, 1846. The Sisters have put up 35,000 papers of seeds for the Western Load." "October 1, 1842. Finish boxing the Western Load. 224

boxes am'ting at $3353.67." (Each fall one or two brethren from New Lebanon peddled seeds across a large territory in upstate New York; that was the Western Load.)

The gardeners must have found great satisfaction in being so productive and making such a big contribution to their society's economy, but their journal entries often have a discouraged tone: "March 13, 1841. The mice have made such dreadful havoc with our seeds that we have become very anxious." "June 12, 1842. A tremendous frost for the time of year, ice thick in standing water. Things in the garden look pretty sorry." "August 23, 1842. Step out into the garden again after being excluded for about a week by wet weather. Some things are nearly rotten, seeds ripening fast, and we found cabbage seed sprouted and indeed with nice green leaves growing in the pods as they grew on the stalk. [We] pull the sugar peas and get them in, a serious job as they were strung up with twine which was difficult to get out." "October 30, 1841. For my part I am quite tired out with such an endless lot of old seeds." (Sorting through unsold seeds returned from the dealers was a particularly unpopular job.) I don't blame the New Lebanon gardeners for complaining. They had to deal with the usual frustrations of gardening—frosts, droughts, storms, insects, vermin, and so on—multiplied by the large scale they were working on, plus the challenges of running a business. And all the while they were trying to live up to Mother Ann's vision of creating a heaven on earth.

WHAT'S INVOLVED IN PRODUCING VEGETABLE SEEDS?
The Shakers wrote very little about the process of raising vegetable seeds. Needless to say, *The Gardener's Manual*, intended to promote seed sales, didn't include a chapter titled "How to Save Your Own Seeds." The garden journal entries noted *when* specific jobs were done but rarely include much explanation about *how* they were done or *why* they were done that way. After the business was established, younger gardeners could learn from the more experienced ones, but I wonder how the first Shaker seed growers got started. Perhaps they had had experience or training in horticulture before joining the faith.

It's not that raising seeds is difficult, but there certainly are some tricks to it, and there's judgment that comes only from experience. The techniques vary from crop to crop. Here's a quick introduction.

Beans and peas are some of the easiest seeds to save. Let the pods ripen on the vines until they turn tan and leathery, then pick them and shell out the seeds. Radishes are almost as easy. A radish plant makes a bushy, branched stalk covered with small stiff pods that ripen in midsummer. Cut the whole stalk or pick individual pods as they turn brown. Crack the pods open to release the seeds. For corn, let the ears mature until the kernels are hard and the husks and stalks turn tan, then pick the ears and store them in a dry place until you can shell the kernels off the cobs.

Winter squash, pumpkin, cantaloupe, and watermelon seeds are mature when the fruit is ripe. Pick out the seeds, wash them in warm water, and spread them out in a very thin layer to dry. Summer squash and cucumbers are usually eaten when they are tender and immature, but if you leave them on the vine for another month or so until the rinds get tough and change color, the seeds inside will be ripe and you can extract and clean them. Likewise, leave eggplants on the plant until the skin is tough, peppers until they turn color, and tomatoes until they are juicy ripe, then sort out the seeds, wash them (save the seeds that sink in water and discard any that float), and spread them out to dry.

Hot weather makes a lettuce plant send up a leafy stalk topped with dozens of flowers that look like miniature dandelions, which bear seeds with dandelion-like plumes. You have to catch these as soon as they ripen or they'll blow away. Spinach also blooms in hot weather, bearing weedy-looking stalks lined with small burs or clusters of seeds. Cut the stalks when they turn tan, let them dry, and rub off the seeds.

The vegetables I've named so far are all annuals that produce seeds in a single growing season. But several of the Shakers' most important crops, including onions, beets, carrots, turnips, parsnips, and cabbages, are biennials. They grow big enough to eat the first year, but they don't flower and set seeds until the second summer. This isn't a problem in mild climates, where you can leave biennials in the ground all winter. In cold climates, though, biennials are liable to freeze outdoors, so the Shakers had to dig up most of their biennial crops in the fall and store them in root cellars for winter protection. Overwintering biennial vegetables is such a critical, challenging, and generally unfamiliar task that Franklin Barber did discuss it explicitly in the New Lebanon garden journal, explaining how to prepare each crop for storage. He noted that "beets keep best in fresh or moist sand. Carrots will rot badly where beets keep well; they should be set in dry sand and put in a dry situation. Turnips and onions, winter radishes, and rutabagas will keep on scaffolds in the cellar. Cabbages should be set up to the neck in moist sand, and the cellar kept just above freezing."

In early spring the Shakers carted all the biennials back out to the garden and replanted them in freshly prepared beds. As their flower stalks developed and grew two to four feet tall, the replanted biennials often got top-heavy, so the gardeners had to use stakes and string to hold the stalks upright until the seeds matured in summer or early fall. Like annuals, biennials die after they produce one crop of seeds and are then discarded.

To achieve their reputation for quality, the Shaker seedsmen paid attention to every step in the process: preparing the soil, raising vigorous seedlings, spacing and thinning to give each plant room to develop, weeding and cultivating regularly, picking the seedpods or fruit at optimum maturity, carefully cleaning and sorting the seeds, drying them quickly, weighing them accurately, and testing their viability (ability to germinate) before selling them. My sense from reading the journals is that even when they were tired, the gardeners were unrelenting in their integrity. They knew how each job should be done, and they worked to do it right.

But there was one job they didn't quite know how to do. A major concern in the seed business is keeping each variety "true to type." A few vegetables, including beans, peas, tomatoes, and peppers, are primarily self-pollinating; their flowers pollinate themselves. With those plants, you can grow two or more varieties side by side without much interbreeding or crossing, and the plants stay pretty much the same generation after generation. Most vegetables, though, are cross-pollinated; their pollen is transferred from flower to flower or plant to plant by insects or by wind. Bees and other insects pollinate cabbage, carrot, onion, lettuce, cucumber, squash, and pumpkin flowers. The pollen of beets, spinach, and corn drifts through the air. Different varieties of a cross-pollinated vegetable can pollinate each other, and when that happens, the offspring are mongrels that may not resemble either parent.

Even botanists didn't know much about pollination or plant breeding in the 1800s, but observant gardeners did realize that crossing occurred. Amelia Simmons, who was not a Shaker (she wrote the first American cookbook, *American Cookery*, which I refer to several times later), noted in 1796 that "all Cabbages will mix, and participate of other species, like Indian Corn....This is new, but a fact." Franklin Barber showed awareness of the problem in his discussion of preparing biennials for winter storage: "Another thing necessary to ensure success in keeping roots and having them reward you for the labor of raising and storing them, is to make a proper selection. The purest and truest after their kind, of all sorts ought always to be selected, this is well known."

Culling the parent plants was an important precaution, but if those plants were cross-pollinated, their seeds—and that's what the Shakers were selling—would not be true to type. Modern seed growers keep cross-pollinated varieties separate and true by planting them at least 200 feet apart (often 1,000 feet or more apart); adjusting the time of planting so different varieties will bloom at different times, not simultaneously; or isolating individual plants or flowers to exclude insects, then pollinating by hand. I haven't seen much evidence that the Shakers took any of these precautions. At New Lebanon they sometimes planted different varieties in adjacent rows and harvested the seeds on consecutive days. But Isaac Hill, editor of *The Farmer's Monthly Visitor*, did describe separate planting in his account of a visit to the Shakers at Alfred, Maine, in 1840: "The persevering attention which the several Societies of Shakers have paid to the production of Garden Seeds for many years, commends them to the public patronage....Of them useful lessons may always be taken in every thing connected with domestic economy and in the productions of the earth. If they raise garden seeds, they know how to preserve the pure varieties of onions, beets, carrots, cabbages, melons, squashes, etc., not suffering them to intermix by growing in near contact."

VEGETABLES IN THE SHAKER DIET

Not all of the Shaker communities were in the vegetable seed business, but they all grew vegetables for their own use, in a kitchen garden that was usually separate from any seed production gardens.

The Shaker diet was not unique. Their ingredients and recipes were typical of their situation and time. Like most middle-class American farmers in the nineteenth century, the Shakers ate plenty of meat, including pork, beef, mutton, fowl, and game; lots of milk, cheese, butter, and other dairy products; bread made from wheat, rye, and cornmeal; oatmeal and other cooked cereals; fresh and dried apples, peaches, pears, cherries, and berries; and various pies, cakes, and other desserts. For vegetables, they had potatoes, onions, beets, turnips, parsnips, carrots, radishes, vegetable oysters or salsify, and other root crops; cabbage, cauliflower, celery, lettuce, spinach, and other greens; fresh and dried peas and beans; sweet corn and dried corn; summer and winter squash and pumpkins; bell peppers, tomatoes, and cucumbers; and asparagus and rhubarb. Special treats, as reported in the Shakers' journal entries, included cantaloupes and watermelons, oranges from Florida, fresh fish (usually caught locally), and clams and other seafood brought inland by train.

That list of foods sounds familiar today, but there are big differences between the early Shaker diet and our modern diet. One difference, of course, is that the Shakers prepared everything "from scratch"; they had no mixes or convenience foods. Just as important are the differences between early and modern food preservation techniques. Canning wasn't invented until the late 1840s. (As usual, the Shakers were quick to adopt the invention. In 1850 Elisha Myrick at Harvard wrote about canning pumpkin, horseradish, and ketchup to sell in Boston.) Home refrigerators didn't replace old-fashioned iceboxes until the early twentieth century, and home freezers followed a few decades later.

Without refrigeration, canning, or freezing, what were the alternatives for vegetable gardeners with short growing seasons? From late May until late September, the Shakers in New York and New England enjoyed vegetables fresh from the garden. Each year's journal entries note the first servings of asparagus, rhubarb, peas, cucumbers, and tomatoes. These seasonal specialties were anticipated and appreciated to a degree we can hardly imagine today. From October through May, there were no vegetables fresh from the garden. From the cellar came potatoes, onions, beets, carrots, other roots, cabbage, celery, and winter squashes. These all store well until Christmas, but start getting stale and flabby after that. From wooden barrels and pottery crocks came pickled cucumbers, pickled beans, pickled beets, pickled peppers, pickled onions, as well as piccalilli and other salty or sour condiments. From bins and bags came dried beans, dried peas, dried sweet corn, and dried pumpkin. Stored, pickled, salted, and dried—those were the options. No wonder people craved a spring tonic of dandelion greens and other wild potherbs in May!

Garden-fresh produce was available for less than half the year. That's one reason early Americans ate fewer vegetables than we do now. Another reason is that most people then were avid meat eaters. Meat was a status food—anyone who could afford to ate it three times a day. By contrast, bread, potatoes, root crops, and cabbage were the staples of poor

67

people. A few prophets denounced such heavy meat eating, but they were often dismissed as spoilsports. Samuel Deane wrote in *The New England Farmer* in 1797 that "[A] kitchen garden is of very considerable importance, as potherbs, salads, and roots of various kinds are useful in housekeeping. Having a plenty of them at hand, a family will not be so likely to run into the errour, which is too common in this country, of eating flesh in too great a proportion for health."

In the 1830s, Sylvester Graham (commemorated in the graham cracker) promoted a diet based on whole-grain bread, a bland gruel of cooked cereal, and vegetables, with no meat at all, minimal butter and cheese, and no coffee or tea. Among other benefits, the Graham diet was supposed to reduce lust, so the celibate Shakers considered it seriously, and some members made a commitment to it. Others did not, though, and dissension between meat eaters and vegetarians polarized some Shaker communities for years. Eventually the meat eaters prevailed. *Mary Whitcher's Shaker House-keeper,* a booklet published by the Shakers in Canterbury, New Hampshire, in 1882 to promote their herbal remedies, includes dozens of recipes for cooking meat (and also for baking all kinds of breads, cakes, pies, puddings, and cookies) but only a few directions for cooking or serving vegetables.

Ironically, *The Gardener's Manual* reveals the ongoing preference for meat in a chapter titled "Of the Uses of Vegetables." You might expect such a chapter to give recipes for salads, soups, casseroles, side dishes, relishes, and such. Instead it describes the benefits of feeding vegetables to livestock: "Carrots are excellent for fattening beef, and for milch cows.... Parsnips are excellent food for cattle, sheep, hogs or horses.... Hogs are said to fatten very easily on them, and to produce superior pork. Cattle are sometimes averse to parsnips at first, but they will soon learn to relish them, after which they will eat them with avidity.... Cabbage leaves, and heads, are excellent for cattle.... Beans are good for Sheep.... Peas, ground up with rye or Indian corn, form a superior provender for fattening hogs." To be fair, that chapter is followed by the chapters "Recipes for Cookery, &c." and "Pickling."

In the nineteenth century some vegetables, such as asparagus, cauliflower, and bell peppers, were picked and served the same way we eat them now. Others were allowed to grow much larger than we're used to seeing them. For example, Samuel Deane described the Scarcity beet, saying, "Ten pounds is the weight of some that I have seen; but in a rich soil, some have grown to two feet in circumference." Amelia Simmons described "middling siz'd" carrots "a foot long and two inches thick at the top end." Mature root vegetables contain more starch than immature ones, so they also last much longer in storage and are more filling and satisfying to hungry eaters. Also, when you're cooking for a large family— especially a Shaker family with up to a hundred people—it's easier to wash, peel, and cut a few foot-long carrots than dozens of little ones. Some peas, beans, and corn were eaten "green" or "new," but most of these crops, too, were allowed to ripen. These seeds develop more starch and more protein as they mature, and only mature seeds dry well for storage. Today we often prefer tender "baby" vegetables, but letting vegetables mature makes good sense nutritionally and horticulturally. It takes hardly any more land or labor to keep a crop growing that extra month or two until it matures, but you harvest considerably more calories and food value.

THE MOST POPULAR SHAKER VEGETABLES

Potatoes. No doubt the Shakers ate more potatoes than any other vegetable. Potatoes were a staple food for all early Americans. Amelia Simmons wrote in *American Cookery* that they "take rank for universal use, profit, and easy acquirement." Potatoes were baked, boiled, fried, made into soups and salads, and mixed with sugar, butter, and eggs to make cakes and puddings. (Simmons gave a recipe for baked potato pudding, made from one pound of boiled potatoes, one pound of sugar, half a pound of butter, and ten eggs!)

Potatoes are easy to grow, and their yield is high. The Shakers treated potatoes as a farm crop, not a garden crop, which meant they grew them by the acre, not by the row. Each community would plant several acres of potatoes and harvest as much as a thousand bushels a year. (Apples were the only other crop to be grown and harvested on that scale.) Several types of potatoes were grown in New England in the 1700s and 1800s, varying in color, size, and shape and in mealiness and flavor, but I haven't seen any references in Shaker writing to the particular types they grew.

Potatoes are normally propagated by planting small tubers, or sections cut from larger tubers; either way, shoots and roots sprout from the "eyes" and develop into new plants. However, potato plants flower abundantly, and they produce true seeds in small fruits that look like green

69

cherry tomatoes. Amelia Simmons in 1796 and Samuel Deane in 1797 both expressed the idea that potatoes tend to deteriorate in quality after several years of replanting the tubers, and that the best way to reinvigorate the stock is to start fresh from seed. Deane recommended gathering the potato fruits in fall, storing them in a frost-free place, mashing out the seeds in spring, sowing them in a hotbed, and transplanting the seedlings to the garden when they are a few inches tall. This works well, but it's a lot more trouble than simply planting tubers, and apparently the idea didn't appeal to the Shakers. They never wrote about gathering or sowing potato seeds, and they never listed potato seeds for sale.

The only mention of potatoes in *The Gardener's Manual* referred to the common practice of growing potatoes as a first crop on newly broken ground, to help break apart the clods of soil: "As gardening should not be undertaken on turf land just broken up, we shall consider the garden free from turf, and considerably ameliorated, as it should be, by a crop of potatoes, or other roots, previous to using it for the rarer kinds of vegetables." Potatoes were so common and familiar that *The Gardener's Manual* didn't have to say any more about them. But *Mary Whitcher's Shaker House-keeper* didn't take potatoes for granted. Mary provided recipes for baked potatoes, potato salad, and "Saratoga Fried Potatoes" (which sound like French fries), and gave a particularly detailed discussion of how to boil potatoes, concluding, "It takes a good cook to boil a potato."

Corn. Like potatoes, corn was a staple for the Shakers, and again they considered it a farm crop, not a garden crop. Corn was indispensable because it was so well adapted to the American climate and gave such high yields. It was sometimes disdained as merely animal food, because so much was fed to livestock, but Samuel Deane testified that "people who are fed on [corn] from their infancy, grow large and strong, and enjoy very good health."

The most common field corns had yellow or white kernels that were starchy, not sweet. These were left on the stalk until fully mature. The dry ripe kernels were ground into corn meal, or Indian meal. Corn meal was cheaper and more common than wheat flour, so corn bread and corn puddings, made from easily memorized recipes, were daily fare. Amelia Simmons's recipe for Johny Cake or Hoe Cake has only three ingredients: "Scald 1 pint of milk and put to 3 pints of Indian meal, and half pint of flower [wheat flour]—bake before the fire." Mary Whitcher's Boiled Indian Pudding is almost as simple: "A cupful of molasses, one of beef suet, chopped fine; four of Indian meal, a little salt, and enough boiling water to make a thick batter. Tie loosely in a cloth, and boil two hours or more. Serve with butter and syrup."

The New Lebanon Shakers in 1843 sold two kinds of corn that were good to eat as corn on the cob in summer and to dry for cooking in winter. As described in *The Gardener's Manual,*

> The Early Canada is the earliest kind of corn we raise, and is preferred only for being several weeks earlier than the common field corn. The Sweet or Sugar Corn is best for cooking in its green state, as it remains much longer in the milk, and is richer and sweeter than any other kind. It is rather later than the common field corn, and is therefore fit for the table when the field corn has become too hard. [Because these varieties ripened at different times, they were unlikely to cross-pollinate each other.] This corn may be preserved for winter use, by parboiling it when green, and cutting it from the cob and drying it in the sun. It then affords a wholesome and agreeable dish when cooked like bean porridge, or what is called *succotash*. Plant the 20th of May, in hills 4 feet distant each way. Cultivate the same as other corn, by ploughing, hilling, &c.

Pumpkins and squash. The Native Americans had developed several types of pumpkins and squash that European settlers were quick to accept as staples in their own diet. Pumpkins were usually grown as field crops, sometimes interplanted with corn and sometimes planted separately. Many of the early breeds of pumpkin had the word "field" in their name, as Connecticut Field, Common Field, or Yankee Field. These were all similar types that produced large rounded or oblong pumpkins with orange rinds and flesh. Pumpkins are easy to grow and prolific, but they don't keep particularly well, and the flesh is usually somewhat watery and stringy when cooked. The Shakers solved the storage problem by peeling, slicing, and drying the pumpkin, making a product called "pumpkin flour," which sounds like the pumpkin equivalent of instant mashed potatoes. Mashed pumpkin was eaten plain or seasoned, or mixed with cream, sugar, eggs, and spices and baked as a custard or pie filling.

71

The New Lebanon Shakers listed four kinds of squash in *The Gardener's Manual*. The Summer Crookneck and Summer Scollop, probably similar to the yellow crookneck and scallop or pattypan squashes we grow today, were boiled, mashed, and served with butter as fresh summer vegetables. The Sweet Potato Squash and Winter Crookneck were large squashes, swollen at the bottom end like pears, with thick mealy flesh and hard rinds, so they could be stored well into the winter. *The Gardener's Manual* noted that the Sweet Potato Squash, cut into pieces and steamed or baked, was considered equal to the Carolina potato or sweet potato (a vegetable the Shakers greatly enjoyed but couldn't produce, because it needs a long, hot growing season). Native Americans ate the seeds of squash and pumpkin, as well as the flesh. The roasted seeds make a tasty and nutritious snack. However, I haven't found any indication that the Shakers took advantage of this resource.

Beans and peas. The Shakers grew several kinds of beans, on both bush and running or pole-type plants. They picked some to eat as green or string beans and let others mature to save as dry beans. *The Gardener's Manual* warned that beans

> are delicate plants, and the seed should not be hurried into the ground till it is well dried and warmed by the sun. The first of May is soon enough in this latitude. (Albany.) The dwarf or bush beans may be sown in drills, 20 inches apart, 2 inches deep, and 6 inches apart in the row. The Running or Pole Beans should be planted in hills, three and a half feet distant each way. We prefer setting the poles before planting. For this purpose we stretch a line, and set the poles by it; then dig and loosen the earth, and drop five or six beans in a circle round the pole, about 3 inches from it, and cover with mellow dirt one inch or one and a half in depth.—When the plants are well up, stir the earth around them, and pull out the weakest plants, leaving three to each hill. This should be done when they are perfectly dry; for beans never should be hoed when wet, nor when any dew is on them [working around wet bean plants can spread foliar fungus diseases].

Nineteenth-century varieties of green beans had tough strings down both sides of the pod that had to be removed before the beans were cooked. Normally they were just boiled and served with butter, but *The Gardener's Manual* suggested that "bean pods, when young and tender may be made very palatable by being firstly boiled, then soaked in vinegar a few hours." Sometimes green beans were preserved by drying the pods, but *The Gardener's Manual* recommended "laying them down in a jar or tub, with a layer of salt between each layer of beans."

The Shakers raised several varieties of dry beans with small or large seeds in various shades of red, pink, brown, tan, and white. To harvest dry beans, they waited until the plants died back (before or after frost), then pulled the vines and brought them indoors to dry. Later they heaped the dry vines on a large sheet of cloth and beat them with a flail to knock the beans out of the pods. Dried beans were soaked overnight, then boiled or baked until they were soft, with some salt pork added for flavoring.

Peas, like beans, were eaten fresh in summer and dried for winter use. In summer the Shakers enjoyed edible-podded or sugar peas, which had thick-walled pods somewhat like today's sugar snap peas, and also fresh green shelled peas, boiled and served with butter. In winter they used dried peas, which were rather starchy and could be green, yellow, or beige, to make stewed peas or pea soup. *Mary Whitcher's Shaker House-keeper* gives a recipe for green pea soup enriched with plenty of cream and milk and thickened like gravy with a roux of butter and flour, and suggests that "a cupful of whipped cream added the last moment is an improvement."

The Gardener's Manual recommended that "late and tall [peas] should be sown in double drills 4 or 5 feet apart, and supported with brush. The early kinds may be sown on ridges at 3 feet distance and a foot high. This will form trenches which will carry off the water and should be kept open at the lower end." Peas, which germinate well while the soil is still cool, were one of the first crops the Shakers planted each spring.

Onions. Onions were very popular in early America and were raised in large quantities starting in the 1600s. On fertile, well-cultivated ground, a crop of onions can be very productive, yielding 500 or more bushels per acre. Some (but not all) kinds keep very well over the winter, and they are indispensable for cooking. The Shakers grew red, yellow, and white onions and ate them boiled, baked, and pickled and used them to season meat and other foods.

The Gardener's Manual gave only brief directions for raising onions from seed: "Sow early in drills, 16 inches apart and half an inch deep. Thin to 4 to 6 inches. The onions will be ripe in September. When the tops are sufficiently dry, pull the onions, and let them lie a few days in the sun to dry; then gather them up and house them." The ease of raising onions *from* seed contrasts with the difficulty of raising onions *for* seed. Onions are biennials. Bulbs stored indoors are replanted the next spring. They send up a stalk in summer topped with a round cluster of starry white flowers, and the seeds ripen in early fall. To achieve maximum seed yield, these second-year onions need ideal conditions—a weed-free plot, well-cultivated soil, prompt removal of any stalks infected with mildew or mold, and careful staking and tying to hold the stalks upright. Perhaps because onion seeds were among their most important and valuable products, the New Lebanon gardeners devoted extra effort and attention to their onion crop and referred to onions frequently in their garden journals.

Cabbage and celery. These two vegetables are unique because they can be stored all winter even though they aren't starchy. Whether served in salads or cooked, their light leafy texture must have been a welcome addition to an otherwise heavy menu.

Cabbage was so common and familiar in early America that neither *The Gardener's Manual* nor *Mary Whitcher's Shaker House-keeper* gave directions or recipes for cooking it or for preparing any kind of slaw or salad; their readers didn't need any advice. Neither booklet gave directions for making sauerkraut, probably because the Shakers came from England, and sauerkraut is a German dish. The New Lebanon Shakers listed five kinds of cabbage in 1843: Early York and Early Sugar Loaf, which formed heads quickly and were eaten fresh in summer; Large Drumhead, which stored well for winter use; Green Savoy, which formed large loose heads of soft-textured, crinkly leaves; and Red Dutch, a red or purple cabbage.

The Gardener's Manual recommended sowing cabbage seeds in a hotbed: "Sow early and late at the same time, thereby to ensure a constant succession of heads; the early furnishing a supply for Fall use, and the late holding out even till the ensuing Spring. As soon as fairly up, thin to 4 inches distance, each way; let them stand here until they have 6 leaves, then transplant. The early kinds, being small, will do at 2 feet apart each way, the late large kinds should have three and a half or four feet." *The Gardener's*

Manual also gave interesting directions for how to store cabbage for winter use, not in a root cellar but outdoors: "Freezing does not hurt Cabbages, provided you can keep them frozen; repeated thawing is what does the mischief. Therefore make a ridge 2 feet high, 6 feet wide, and as long as you need, on the north side of a building; on this lay some poles crosswise, and on the poles some narrow boards lengthwise, 2 inches apart. Take up your Cabbages in a dry day, just before Winter, strip off some of the outside leaves, and set them, roots upward, on the boards, cover them a foot deep with straw or corn stalks, and they will keep fresh and green." This was valuable advice for home gardeners, who usually had limited space in their root cellars.

One last note on cabbage. As noted previously, it is biennial, so to produce seeds the Shakers had to raise heads one year, store them in a root cellar, then set them out again in spring. The flower stalks develop from buds on the core, deep inside the head, but if the head is too tight, the stalks cannot emerge. So the gardener has to serve as midwife, cutting a shallow cross in the top of the head. According to journal entries, the Shaker seed gardeners made this cut in late spring, about four to six weeks after setting out the plants. Once they emerge, the bushy, branching flower stalks quickly grow two to four feet tall, bearing thousands of yellow flowers like mustard blossoms that ripen into slender seedpods.

Few gardeners today have seen the flowers of common cabbage, and you might be confused by the appearance of another plant called flowering cabbage or flowering kale. Flowering cabbage is an ornamental (it is edible, however, and is often used as a garnish) that forms a loose head of fluffy, ruffled leaves in bright shades of pink, lavender, purple, and white. It looks like a giant rose, but that "rose" is all leaves. Flowering cabbage belongs to the same species (*Brassica oleracea*) as other cabbages and forms its *real* flowers just as they do, in its second year.

Celery isn't related to cabbage at all, but I put it here because both are strong-flavored, crisp-textured leafy vegetables that can be stored through the winter. You really have to appreciate celery to bother growing it. It's a prima donna crop that needs excellent soil and regular attention throughout the growing season. *The Gardener's Manual* explained that celery "is prepared for the table by bleaching." To do this, you dig trenches eighteen inches wide and eighteen inches deep, layer rotten manure and rich soil in the bottom, then set the celery plants (started months earlier in a hotbed and already transplanted once to a cooler nursery bed) in a line along the center of the trench. "When they have attained the height of ten inches, you may commence earthing them up.... In performing this, care should be taken to gather all the leaves up with the hand while drawing the earth up equally on each side of the row, being careful to leave the hearts of the plants open. Repeat the earthing once a week or oftener, till about the last week in October. From this time it will not grow much, but it is best to let it stand out till the ground is about to be locked up by frost, then dig it and pack it away in the cellar. It will keep till May."

Beets, carrots, turnips, and other root crops. Root crops were important because they store well, are relatively easy to grow, and are quite productive. Carrots, for example, can yield several hundred bushels per acre. The New Lebanon Shakers in 1843 listed six kinds of beets: early and late, large and larger, starchy and sugary, with red, white, and yellow flesh; three kinds of carrots, including the Long Orange, which grew quite long and large; five kinds of radishes, including tender summer radishes and larger, tougher, thicker-skinned winter radishes; three kinds of turnips; rutabaga or yellow turnip, which has yellow instead of white flesh; parsnip, which is like a sweet white carrot; and salsify, or vegetable oyster, which has long thin roots.

The Gardener's Manual gives very brief directions for growing these root crops: just sow the seeds in rows about eighteen inches apart, and thin the seedlings four to six inches apart. There are a few additional comments. For parsnips, "In November dig enough for winter use, and put in the cellar; let the rest stand in the ground till spring." Radishes "should be sown once a fortnight, in order to have a supply through the season." Salsify "is highly esteemed by those best acquainted with it.... It is very excellent boiled and mashed up like squash and turnip, with a little salt and butter. Some make soup of it.... Others prefer it parboiled, and then sliced up and fried in batter, or without." Beets can be pickled: "Boil them, scrape off the skin, and soak them in vinegar 24 hours, or till wanted for use. When thus prepared they form an excellent substitute for pickled cucumbers." Most of the time beets, carrots, and other roots were simply boiled and served with butter, salt, and pepper.

Lettuce, spinach, and other greens. The New Lebanon Shakers listed six kinds of lettuce seeds in 1843, including looseleaf and head types, and recommended sowing lettuce at regular intervals throughout the season. I assume they ate lots of lettuce salads in summer, but I don't know what they used for salad dressings. I wonder if they served lettuce separately or combined it with other raw vegetables. Nothing I've read gives any insight on the topic of Shaker salads.

The Shakers also sold peppergrass or curled cress (described in *The Gardener's Manual* as "an agreeable salad"), parsley ("a salutary pot herb"), and spinach (no comments on how to grow or use it). I expect that spinach was usually—you guessed it—boiled and served with butter, salt, and pepper. Among settlers of English descent, "potherb" was a general term for spinach, parsley, mustard greens, dandelion leaves, beet and turnip leaves, purslane tops, and other garden and wild plants that were cooked separately or together as "a mess of pottage." Amelia Simmons's *American Cookery* explained the fine points of preparing potherbs in her directions for boiling "all kinds of Garden Stuff." She wrote: "In dressing all sorts of kitchen garden herbs, take care they are clean washed; that there be no small snails, or caterpillars between the leaves; and that all the coarse outer leaves, and the tops that have received any injury by the weather, be taken off; next wash them in a good deal of water, and put them into a cullender to drain, care must likewise be taken, that your pot or sauce pan be clean, well tinned, and free from sand, or grease."

Asparagus. The Shakers loved asparagus, partly because it was one of the very first vegetables of spring. Asparagus is a perennial, and once established, the same patch can be harvested for decades, with no annual maintenance except cutting or burning down the old stalks in spring and spreading a top dressing of manure in summer. *The Gardener's Manual* noted that asparagus "is a very delicious esculent vegetable, and easily cultivated, after the first operation of preparing the ground. It is sown the first year, and transplanted the second" into soil tilled eighteen inches deep and amended with "a bountiful supply of strong manure." "The buds or young shoots, which is the part used, will be fit for cutting the third year; they should be cut sparingly the first year, but thereafter, the cutting may be continued until the first of July." When boiling asparagus, "Be careful to take up the stalks as soon as they become tender, so as to preserve their true flavor and green color; for boiling a little too long will destroy both.

Serve up with melted butter or cream."

The Shakers also sold seeds for sea kale (*Crambe maritima*), a hardy perennial vegetable that's rarely grown today, noting, "This is a capital article; the cultivation and use are the same as those of Asparagus." *The Gardener's Manual* didn't elaborate beyond this, but English gardening books all emphasize the need to blanch the stalks of sea kale as they emerge in spring, by covering them with an inverted flowerpot or pulling dirt around them. This makes the stalks white and tender like asparagus; otherwise they turn green and get tough and bitter.

Tomatoes. Although some Americans knew of tomatoes in the early 1800s, they didn't eat them then. At that time, tomatoes were grown as ornamentals, if at all, and considered poisonous. Only a few decades later, though, their edibility was established and they assumed an important role in the American diet. The New Lebanon Shakers listed one variety, Large Red tomato, in 1843, and *The Gardener's Manual* told how to grow it: "They should be sown in the hot-bed in April, and when the ground becomes warm, and the danger from frost is over, they may be transplanted out, 4 or 5 feet distant each way. The fruit will ripen better if the vines are supported by a trellis, or something similar, to elevate them from the ground a little."

The Gardener's Manual offered some suggestions for readers who didn't know how to use their tomatoes. It told how to prepare a "tomato catchup or catsup" which makes "an excellent sauce or gravy for meat or fish," how to preserve fresh tomatoes "by covering them in sugar," how to make tomato pickles seasoned with mustard, black pepper, horseradish, and cloves, and how to prepare stewed tomatoes topped with bread or cracker crumbs. Better yet, here's a recipe for tomato pie from *Mary Whitcher's Shaker House-keeper*: "Peel and slice ripe tomatoes and sprinkle over them a little salt. Let them stand a few minutes; then pour off the juice, and add sugar, half a cupful of cream, one egg, and nutmeg, and cover with a paste [crust]. Bake in a moderate oven over half an hour. This makes an excellent and much-approved pie."

Peppers and eggplant. These vegetables are related to the tomato, and while they never shared the stigma of being considered poisonous, they never became as popular, either. *The Gardener's Manual* named three kinds of sweet peppers and recommended that "these should be sown in the hot bed in April, and transplanted out the first of June, 2 feet distant each way." It stated that "sweet peppers are commonly used, when fully ripe, as a salad [whatever that means]; or the core may be extracted and the cavity filled with mince meat, which, on being thus baked, receives a very agreeable relish." To pickle peppers, "Pick them while in a green state, and put them into a strong cold brine [salt water]. Before eating, soak them in cold water 24 hours, and sour them at pleasure."

For eggplant, *The Gardener's Manual* recommended, "Sow the seeds in March, in a hot bed, and plant them out towards the latter part of May, in a rich, warm piece of ground.... [Their fruit], if rightly prepared, is by many esteemed equal to eggs. Some are very fond of them when sliced and fried with ham." *The Gardener's Manual* gave a recipe for fried eggplant that is unusual, because very few nineteenth-century Shaker recipes called for herbs. Here it is: "Cut [the eggplant] into slices about a quarter of an inch thick, put them into a dish, and pour on boiling water, let them remain a minute or two; drain off the water, and season with pepper and salt, or with thyme, marjoram, or summer savory, according to the palate to be suited; dust them with flour and put them into a frying pan, which should be ready with hot beef drippings, or lard. When browned on one side, turn them and brown the other."

Cucumbers and melons. Judging from journal entries, fresh cucumbers, muskmelons, and watermelons were some of the Shakers' favorite summer treats. The first serving of cucumbers was noted almost every summer, and a serving of melons was a veritable holiday. Melons were such a treat that the Millennial Laws included a special warning that "melons, & other choice or uncommon fruits, should be equally divided to the family, as far as consistent; and no member should raise or gather them...to give to particular individuals to court favor or affection."

Cucumbers and melons were eaten fresh as long as they were available. *Mary Whitcher's Shaker House-keeper* offered these directions for keeping them a little longer: "When cucumbers are in their best they should be cut and laid in a box just to fit them, and then bury the box in some dry sand, covering it over to the depth of a foot. There should not be any hay or moss with them in the box, as it will cause them to turn yellow. If laid in a box without hay or moss, the color and bloom may be preserved

79

for two weeks to look as fresh as the day they were cut. Melons may also be kept in the same way." Of course, cucumbers were pickled for winter use, and *The Gardener's Manual* gave two methods for pickling them, in salt brine or in vinegar. Melons can be pickled, too: Amelia Simmons's *American Cookery* told how to "pickle or make mangoes" of green melons seasoned with garlic, ginger, nutmeg, and black pepper and stuffed with a startling measure of mustard seeds.

The New Lebanon Shakers listed four kinds of cucumbers and three kinds of melons in 1843. A decade later the Shakers in Enfield, Connecticut, listed nine kinds of cucumbers and nineteen kinds of melons. The Enfield Shakers were known for their melon seeds and for their melons. Enfield has a longer, warmer growing season than most of New England, and melons like that. *The Gardener's Manual* gave brief directions for raising these crops: "The 20th of May is soon enough to plant cucumbers here. Hills to be 4 feet distant each way. One plant is enough for a hill, ultimately; but to make provision for insects, plenty of seed should be put in, and the plants afterwards thinned out." "Musk melons require the same treatment as cucumbers. Watermelons should be planted further apart. A shovel full of ashes applied to each hill and mixed with the soil is beneficial."

Nasturtiums. Gardeners today often grow cheerful, long-flowering nasturtiums to decorate their vegetable gardens, but the ever-utilitarian Shakers grew them to eat, as *The Gardener's Manual* explained: "This is an annual plant, a native of Peru, and is much cultivated for the berries, which if gathered while green and pickled in vinegar, make a good substitute for capers. Sow as early as the season will admit, in drills an inch deep. The plants should be supported from the ground by bushy sticks, or otherwise, in order to have them do well and produce a plentiful crop of good fruit.... [The] berries must be gathered when they have just attained their full size, and while they are green, plump, and tender. Spice the vinegar, and pour it on hot."

Winter squashes with hard rinds and thick, mealy flesh can be stored well into the winter. Bees carry pollen from one squash blossom to another. This kind of cross-pollination was a problem for the Shakers, who tried to keep their seeds pure and "true to type."

Cabbage was an essential crop, because it's one of the few leafy vegetables that can be stored through the winter months.

The Shakers grew several kinds of beets, with red, yellow, or white flesh.

Asparagus forms small red berries that ripen in fall. The Shakers collected these berries, then extracted and sold the seeds.

Formerly considered poisonous, tomatoes became a very popular vegetable by the mid-1800s.

*Today we grow nasturtium for its flowers, but the Shakers considered it
a vegetable and pickled its plump, peppery-flavored seedpods.*

This equipment at
Hancock Shaker Village
recalls the Shakers' preparation
of herbs and plants for
pharmaceutical purposes.
Several communities raised
medicinal plants. They also
collected wild roots and
tree bark from the woods
surrounding their villages.

The Shakers grew more sage than any other herb, harvesting and drying the fragrant leaves.

The Shakers used tea brewed from mother-of-thyme for upset stomaches and headaches.

Today we use basil as a seasoning. Traditionally it was used in medicine.

OPPOSITE PAGE:
In hot weather, lettuce plants send up leafy stalks that bear yellow flowers and dandelion-like seeds. The Shakers gathered and sold lettuce seeds, and they also made an extract from lettuce plants that was used as a substitute for opium.

The opium poppy is a beautiful plant, with broad flowers and unusual blue-green foliage.

Horseradish roots, boiled in brown sugar syrup, made a traditional cough remedy.

THE SHAKER MEDICINAL
PLANT INDUSTRY

Why send to Europe's distant shores
For plants which grow at our own doors?
—TITLE PAGE, NEW LEBANON MEDICINAL PLANTS CATALOG

SHAKER COOKS in the nineteenth century made little use of culinary
herbs. They relied mostly on salt and pepper for seasoning main dishes
and used cinnamon, cloves, ginger, and other imported spices for
desserts. The few herbs they did use were the same ones that Amelia
Simmons had described in *American Cookery* in 1796: "Thyme is good
in soups and stuffings. Sweet Marjoram is used in Turkeys. Summer
Savory, ditto, and in sausages and salted Beef, and legs of Pork. Sage is
used in Cheese and Pork, but not generally approved. Parsley is good
in soups, and to garnish roast Beef, and is excellent with bread and
butter in the spring. Sweet Thyme is most useful and best approved
in cookery."

The Shakers sold cans of dried sage, summer savory, sweet
marjoram, and thyme (parsley doesn't dry well). Several communities
also sold seeds of these five herbs, plus seeds of various other herbs,
including caraway, cayenne pepper, clary sage, coriander, dill, fennel,
hyssop, lavender, lemon balm, pot marigold (now called calendula),
rosemary, rue, American saffron (actually safflower), salad burnet, sorrel,
and sweet basil. Overwhelmingly, though, the Shakers were known not
for their culinary herbs, nor for their herb seeds, but for their extensive
line of medicinal herb products.

Starting about 1820 and continuing through the century, they
sold hundreds of kinds of dried herbs, herb extracts, herb oils, and
herbal patent medicines, earning an income that rivaled or exceeded that
from the vegetable seed business. The New Lebanon community ran the

largest medicinal plant business, followed by the communities at Harvard, Massachusetts; Canterbury, New Hampshire; Watervliet, New York; and Union Village, Ohio; a few other communities participated on a smaller scale or for a shorter time period.

There are many parallels between the Shakers' medicinal herb business and their vegetable seed business. In both cases they were pioneers who developed a desirable product just as the market for it was beginning to boom and soon achieved a reputation for quality, purity, neatness, honesty, and fairness. Both businesses required careful knowledge of plants, hard labor in the field, plenty of hands for sorting and packing the products, and willingness to invent or adopt labor-saving devices to facilitate the process. And production of both herbs and seeds peaked around midcentury and declined afterward as society changed and as the Shakers encountered more and more competition while their own population and labor pool kept shrinking.

AMERICAN MEDICINE IN THE NINETEENTH CENTURY

To put the Shaker herb business in perspective, it helps to look at the big picture. Americans in the nineteenth century had, for the most part, different health problems than we have today. Burns, falls, and accidental injuries were often crippling. Birth defects were lifelong handicaps. Many women died in childbirth, and many children died in infancy. Those who survived were vulnerable to colds and flus that could lead to pneumonia and to contagious diseases such as tuberculosis, smallpox, scarlet fever, typhoid fever, yellow fever, and cholera. Eating rancid or spoiled food (there was no refrigeration, of course) or excessive amounts of meat or greasy food caused both acute and chronic digestive disorders. Eating too much salt pork and other foods preserved or heavily seasoned with salt caused fluid retention or dropsy and high blood pressure. Children and adults often carried intestinal parasites, or "worms." Malaria was a problem in swampy regions where mosquitoes swarmed. Simple cuts, punctures, and other wounds easily became critically infected. Boils and sores could develop into persistent cankers. Some people suffered from asthma or allergies. Others developed arthritis or rheumatism. There were ailments with names you never hear of now, like gleet, phthisis, quinsy, and tetter.

Facing problems like that, what could doctors do? At first they couldn't do much. In 1800 doctors had virtually no understanding of what caused diseases or how to prevent them. They had no awareness of bacteria, no understanding of how contagious diseases were transmitted, scant appreciation for sanitation or hygiene, no knowledge of nutrition, and no explanation for congenital disorders. They had no antiseptics, no antibiotics, no vaccines, no anesthetics, and only a few painkillers. Much of this had changed by 1900. The nineteenth century was one of great transition—and much turmoil—in medicine. The rise and fall of the Shaker herb business makes sense when you view it in this context.

In 1800 the champion of the medical establishment was Dr. Benjamin Rush, who taught more than 2,000 doctors during his forty-four-year tenure at the University of Pennsylvania. Following the tradition of English and European doctors since the 1600s, Rush practiced "heroic" medicine, believing that "desperate diseases call for desperate remedies." Heroic doctors used a few plant medicines— rhubarb root and other cathartics and emetics, Peruvian bark (quinine) for malarial fevers, opium as a sedative and painkiller, and occasional doses of foxglove, aconite, poison hemlock, belladonna, and henbane— all dangerously potent plants. Beyond that, these doctors mostly used drastic procedures, primarily bloodletting and purges, to expel diseased matter from the body. In particular, Rush advocated the use of calomel (mercurous chloride), an extremely poisonous compound that immediately purged the body. Rush called calomel "a safe and nearly universal medicine," despite the fact that it caused serious long-term damage, including chronic profuse salivation and grotesque facial disfiguration. Considering the nature of these treatments, you might wonder who was the hero in heroic medicine—the doctor or any patient who managed to survive?

Many patients avoided conventional doctors, fearful of the treatment they might receive. Others couldn't reach or afford these doctors, most of whom practiced in cities and treated middle-class or wealthy patients. People who couldn't or wouldn't go to doctors could use herbal remedies prepared at home or seek help from local men or women who were unlicensed but had gained a reputation for healing. In the early 1800s some of the most effective of these local "root and herb" doctors were those who had studied with Native American healers and had started using native medicinal plants in their practice along with traditional European herbs.

This growing awareness of and appreciation for native medicinal plants was a challenge to conventional medicine. But nothing could stop the trend or stop the presses; many books were being published to promote the uses of these plants. One of the first to gain widespread recognition was *The Indian Doctor's Dispensatory* by Peter Smith, published in 1813. Smith had received a classical education and was trained in standard medical practice, but he called himself an Indian doctor because, after studying with the Indians, he felt that "the natives of our own country are in possession of cures, simples &c. that surpass what is used by our best practitioners."

Following the European tradition, heroic doctors thought that "irregular arterial action" was the cause of most disease. Like most Native Americans, Smith believed that "obstructed perspiration [is] the real first cause of half the diseases of the human body." When you catch a cold, and your skin becomes dry, he said, one thing leads to another, and soon a minor ailment becomes a major illness. To prevent this, "Drink sage tea (or any other warming, sweating tea will do, such as pennyroyal, mint, sassafras, or dogwood buds) copiously and go to bed, and drink it, hot or cold, but not very strong, until you bring yourself into a little sweat, then go to sleep and you may expect to wake up well." Smith's book described a few dozen herbs, often quite vividly; gave the properties and dosage for each; and proposed cures for asthma, itching, broken bones, piles, nosebleed, and other conditions. Smith also recommended hydrotherapy (washing) for many injuries; in 1813, washing a wound with clean water was a novel suggestion!

Another book popular at that time was *Every man his own doctor; or, a treatise on the prevention and cure of diseases, by regimen and simple medicines. To which is added, a Treatise on the Materia Medica, in which the medicinal qualities of indigenous plants are given and adapted to common practice,* by William Buchan, M.D. Buchan identified many causes of disease—everything from wet feet and damp beds to passions, infections, and bad air. He recommended attention to diet and sanitation as a way to prevent disease, and he discussed the medical uses of dozens of native and naturalized European plants. Among other remedies, Buchan recommended two plants—yellow wild indigo (*Baptisia tinctoria*) and horehound (*Marrubium vulgare*)—for relieving the symptoms of mercury poisoning in patients who had received heroic treatment, and he cited ground ivy (*Glechoma hederacea*) for relief of lead colic—a chronic and painful constipation suffered by almost all painters in the days when most paint contained lead.

Two major works were published in 1817, one written by Dr. William Barton, a famous botanist and a respected friend and colleague of Dr. Benjamin Rush, and the other by Dr. James Bigelow, a professor at Harvard. Both works were titled *Vegetable Materia Medica of the United States*, and several of the same plants appeared in each. Both were expensive, large-format, beautifully illustrated books designed to appeal to the middle and upper classes. The status of the authors and the quality of the presentation affirmed that our native plants had "arrived" on the medical scene.

Another milestone in 1817 was the first edition of Amos Eaton's *Manual of Botany for the Northern and Middle States of America, containing generic and specific descriptions of the indigenous plants and common cultivated exotics, growing north of Virginia.* Eaton was a professor of botany and chemistry in the Vermont Medical Institution, which was connected with Middlebury College in Vermont, not far from the New Lebanon Shakers in New York. Eaton's descriptions are terse, with many abbreviations and few comments, but the Shakers quickly adopted his *Manual* as their authority for plant names. They may have known and respected Eaton personally, and they surely would have appreciated the quotation, attributed to Linnaeus, which he chose for the title page: "That existence is surely contemptible, which regards only the gratification of instinctive wants and the preservation of a body made to perish."

Finally, and perhaps of greatest significance to the Shakers, was *Medical Flora, or Manual of the Medical Botany of the United States in North America*, by an eccentric but extremely hard-working and productive botanist, Constantine S. Rafinesque. This work was published in two compact, affordable volumes in 1828 and 1830. Rafinesque tooted his own horn in the introduction, praising his work by comparison to the fancier and more expensive books by Barton and Bigelow, and proclaiming that "works of general utility ought to be accurate, complete, portable, and cheap. Such alone can spread the required correct knowledge, and suit every class of readers.... It is time that we should return to the pristine Linnean simplicity, and by the addition of cheap but correct figures...speak to the eyes as well as the mind." His two volumes are substantial, pleasant to hold, and nicely illustrated with realistic botanical drawings printed in bright green ink! He discussed scores of plants in considerable detail. The Shakers greatly admired Rafinesque's attitude and his knowledge; he in turn praised the Shakers on many occasions.

There were many other books, but the ones I have mentioned were particularly important to the Shakers and to the growth of their medicinal herb industry. As stated in the catalogs from the Watervliet Shakers: "There are many [native herbs] worthy of trial of physicians.... For a full description of the properties of many active medicinal plants indigenous to our country, see Rafinesque, Barton, Bigelow, etc.,...where it will be found that the use of many foreign drugs may be advantageously superseded by our own native remedies."

Along with the growing appreciation for native remedies, two related movements, started by two distinctly colorful characters, combined to topple the traditional practice of heroic medicine. The first character was Samuel Thomson, who developed a system called Thomsonian medicine. Many of his ideas came indirectly from Native American practices, which he learned secondhand; he spent much of his childhood scouring the woods and fields with a family friend, the widow Benton, who healed with "roots and herbs, applied to the patient, or given in hot drinks, to produce sweating; which always answered the purpose. When one thing did not produce the desired effect, she would try something else, till they were relieved." As a boy, Thomson discovered the powerful effects of a modest-looking annual weed, *Lobelia inflata*. As he later wrote:

> This plant is what I have called the Emetic Herb, and is the most important article I make use of in my practice. It is very common in most parts of this country, and may be prepared and used in almost any manner....There is no danger to be apprehended from its use, as it is perfectly harmless in its operation, even when a large quantity is taken—it operates as an emetic, cleanses the stomach from all improper aliment, promotes an internal heat, which is immediately felt at the

extremities, and produces perspiration. . . . I feel perfectly convinced from near thirty years experience of its medical properties, that the discovery is of incalculable importance and if properly understood by the people, will be more useful in curing the diseases incident to their climate, than the drugs and medicines sold by all the apothecaries in the country.

Thomson thought that "cold, or want of heat" is the cause of "all disorders which the human family are afflicted with, however various the symptoms, and different the names by which they are called." The system of Thomsonian medicine centered on "courses of therapy" designed to "restore vital heat." These courses included lobelia purges to empty the system, sweetened gruels to restore the digestion, steam baths to warm the body and increase perspiration, and hot teas of red pepper and other strong herbs. Applying what he had learned from the widow Benton, Thomson used dozens of other herbs to supplement or vary the basic treatment. The purges and red-pepper tea sound unpleasant, but Thomson's patients were extremely grateful and loyal to him, and they testified to his sympathy, consideration, and excellent bedside manner. Most important, most of his patients recovered, and his treatments did no harm.

Thomson was at odds with the medical establishment. When he was granted a meeting with Dr. Rush, he expressed his opinion of "the absurdity of bleeding to cure disease; and pointed out its inconsistency, in as much as the same method was made use of to cure a sick man and to kill a well beast." Regular doctors berated him and tried to discredit him, but he persevered, traveling widely to lecture, heal, and gain converts. He patented his system, licensed agents to practice it; wrote the *New Guide to Health* or *Botanic Family Physician*, which went through several editions in the 1820s and 1830s; and claimed more than three million supporters by 1839. (He then became cantankerous, and the whole business was in disarray when he died in 1843.) Thomson's ideas greatly influenced the Shakers. According to medical historian J. Worth Estes, "The handwritten volumes of medical recipes compiled for everyday use in Shaker villages contain many Thomsonian remedies. . . . Several Shaker-made remedies were designed in the Thomsonian tradition, even if they were not explicitly labeled as such."

"Irregular arterial activity," "obstructed perspiration," "cold, or want of heat"—there were several conflicting explanations for disease in the early 1800s. What remained was for someone to piece these together into a more comprehensive system. This was the vision of Wooster Beach. As a young man, Beach first studied with an old "root and herb" doctor who taught him about Indian remedies and European herbs. Beach criticized much of traditional medicine, but he went on to earn an M.D. degree, hoping to change the system from the inside. Finding his efforts unwelcome, he started his own system, the Reformed Practice of Medicine, or Eclecticism, and opened a medical school in New York City. Beach's idea was to combine the best of traditional medicine (while avoiding its excesses, such as bloodletting and the use of calomel) with the extensive use of a wide variety of herbs. Beach was more of a scientist than a leader, and the Eclectic movement soon grew out of his control, spreading throughout the eastern United States and England. Starting in the 1830s, several colleges of Eclectic medicine were founded, and they awarded thousands of degrees. Some of these degrees were bogus—the schools were often underfunded and ill equipped—and some Eclectic doctors were little more than snake-oil salesmen, with patent remedies for every ailment known to man.

But Eclectic medicine, like Thomsonian medicine, which it encompassed after Thomson died, created a big demand for medicinal herbs, and the Shaker herb industry grew in proportion to the influence of these movements. Along with hundreds of "generic" dried herbs and herb extracts, the Shakers were glad to produce "brand-name" products. Catalogs from Canterbury, for example, noted that "botanical practitioners are hereby informed that the various simples and compounds introduced by Beach, Howard, Thompson, Smith, and others, are prepared with fidelity and care, and sold on terms corresponding with prices in the general Catalogue."

After the Civil War, the Eclectics lost influence as conventional medicine began to modernize and gain respect, and as a proliferation of patent medicines promised relief from any and all ailments, as we'll see later.

HOW THE SHAKERS HEALED THEMSELVES

The earliest Shakers, especially when Mother Ann was still alive, relied on faith healing and the laying on of hands to relieve all but the most drastic illnesses and injuries, and called on worldly doctors only as a last resort.

Starting in the 1820s, however, they acknowledged the limitations of faith healing and set up their own infirmaries, and each family designated men and women to serve as physicians to the brethren and sisters—treated separately, of course. A few of the men already had medical training when they joined the society, and a few who had grown up in the society were sent off to medical school, but most of the men and nearly all of the women who served as Shaker physicians learned on the job and trained themselves by studying whatever books were available.

Individual Shakers often had strong preferences for one system or another, but as a group the Shakers were more eclectic than the Eclectics. They tried everything: faith healing, heroic remedies, emetics, purges, vapor baths, steam inhalation, mineral springs, hot and cold wraps, herbal poultices and blisters, herbal teas, fasting, special diets, electrotherapy (the application of a low-voltage direct current), even horticultural therapy. The garden journal from New Lebanon noted that one brother, "being rather unwell or debilitated from hard labor, seeks an asylum in the garden with a view to regain his vigor and renovate his system" and later named another whose "health of late is quite miserable, and for the purpose of finding better he leaves the tailoring trade and comes into the garden; to do what little he can amongst the seeds and dirt."

In general, though, the Shakers emphasized prevention rather than treatment, and they often maintained excellent health into old age. They followed a regular routine with scheduled times for exercise and rest, diligently pursued cleanliness and hygiene, ate three meals a day, breathed fresh air, drank pure water, and used little if any alcohol or tobacco. A little booklet called *Simple Wisdom* summed up the basics of healthy living for Shakers: stay warm, eat regularly and slowly, keep your skin clean, get plenty of sleep, be cheerful, avoid debt, and don't covet unneeded things.

AN OVERVIEW OF THE SHAKER HERB INDUSTRY
In the early 1800s the Shakers at all communities collected herbs for their own use and may have sold a few from time to time, but the herb business, and the practice of extensively cultivating herbs rather than collecting them from the wild, didn't take off until 1820 at New Lebanon. An article published in 1852 in the *American Journal of Pharmacy* quoted Edward Fowler, a trustee at New Lebanon:

It is about fifty years since our Society first originated... a business of cultivating and preparing medicinal plants for the supply and convenience of apothecaries and druggists, [but it began] on a limited scale. [About 1820] Drs. E. Harlow and G. K. Lawrence, of our Society, the latter an excellent botanist, gave their attention to the business, and induced a more systematic arrangement, and scientific manner of conducting it, especially as to the seasons for collection, varieties, and method of preparation. Since their time, the business has rapidly increased, and especially so within the last ten years. We believe the quantity of botanical remedies used in this country, particularly of indigenous plants, has doubled in less than that time.

Fowler continued:

There are now probably occupied as physic gardens in the different branches of our Society, nearly two hundred acres, of which about fifty are at our village. As we find a variety of soils are necessary to the perfect production of the different plants, we have taken advantage of our farms and distributed our gardens accordingly. Hyoscyamus [henbane], belladonna, taraxacum [dandelion], aconite, poppies, lettuce, sage, summer savory, marjoram, dock, burdock, valerian, and horehound, occupy a large portion of the ground; and about fifty minor varieties are cultivated in addition.... Of indigenous plants we collect about two hundred varieties, and purchase from the South, and West, and from Europe, some thirty or forty others.

In an article in *Harper's* magazine in July 1857, Benson Lossing reported on the New Lebanon herb business, which was at its peak in the 1850s; up to 100,000 pounds of dried herbs and several thousand pounds of extracts were produced annually. The article described the Herb House as a frame building 120 feet long by 40 feet wide, with two stories plus a full basement and attic. "The second story and attic are the drying rooms, where the green herbs are laid upon sheets of canvas, [stacked] about fourteen inches apart, supported by cords." Lossing commented on the horse-powered press, which could process 250 pounds of herbs (leaves and tops) or 600 pounds of roots daily into "solid cakes, an inch thick, and seven and a quarter inches square, weighing a pound each," and noted that "about ten persons are continually employed in this business, and occasionally twice that number are there."

The Extract House was a frame building 36 feet wide by 100 feet long, "supplied with the most perfect apparatus.... In the principal room of the laboratory the chief operations of cracking, steaming, and pressing the roots and herbs are carried on, together with the boiling of the juices thus extracted." The juices were then distilled in a copper vacuum pan to make concentrated extracts. (In 1853 Gail Borden copied the Shakers' vacuum pan, which they hadn't patented, and used a similar process to make Borden's Condensed Milk.)

In another room, dried roots were "ground between giant granite stones into a fine powder." Finally, "in another building is the Finishing Room, where the various products are labeled and packed for market." Lossing noted that "in every department perfect order and neatness prevail. System is everywhere observed, and all operations are carried on with exact economy."

From the 1830s to the 1870s, the New Lebanon Shakers issued several herb catalogs with impressive titles like this, from 1851: *A Catalogue of Medicinal Plants, Barks, Roots, Seeds, Flowers and Select Powders with their Therapeutic Qualities and Botanical names; also Pure Vegetable Extracts, prepared in vacuo; Ointments, Inspissated Juices, Essential Oils, Double Distilled and Fragrant Waters, etc. etc., Raised, Prepared and Put up in the most Careful Manner by the United Society of Shakers at New Lebanon, NY.* That catalog listed 356 medicinal herbs, 4 common culinary herbs, and 181 fluid extracts, along with much more, and carried this endorsement from Constantine Rafinesque: "The best medical gardens in the United States are those established by the communities of the Shakers,...who cultivate and collect a great variety of medical plants. They sell them cheap, fresh and genuine."

I don't know what select powders were, but if you're wondering about those inspissated juices, they were condensed or thickened extracts, made in this case specifically from poisonous plants. The fragrant waters were distilled from roses, peach leaves, sassafras bark, peppermint and spearmint, elder flowers, and other plants, and used as flavorings and perfumes. The extracts and ointments were sold in small glass or ceramic bottles and jars. Most of the dried herbs and roots were pressed into blocks, as Lossing described, then wrapped in pastel papers, with simple labels pasted on the outside.

As with their vegetable seeds, in marketing their herb products, the Shakers emphasized accurate identification, freshness, purity, quality, neatness, and respect for the customer. Again, as with the seeds, some herb products were sold directly to individual buyers, but most went to wholesale agents, retail druggists, or doctors. The Shakers shipped herbs throughout the United States and overseas.

Besides the community at New Lebanon, the other big producers of medicinal herbs were Harvard, Union Village, Canterbury, and Watervliet; the two Enfields (in Connecticut and Massachusetts) and New Gloucester (now Sabbathday Lake) were involved on a smaller scale. They all issued one or more catalogs during the decades from 1830 to 1880. Most of the catalogs have a similar look, listing hundreds of plants by their common and Latin names, with price per pound and brief abbreviations indicating each plant's medicinal properties. Some include lists of synonymous common names, expanded descriptions of the most popular products, or other features.

Amy Bess Miller, author of *Shaker Herbs*, studied account books from New Lebanon, Harvard, Union Village, Canterbury, and Watervliet and determined that during its peak decades, the herb business at these societies "was averaging an aggregate gross of at least $150,000 annually." With that kind of potential income, why didn't all the other Shaker communities join the herb business too? A major reason, I think, was the challenge of selecting, training, and retaining qualified brethren to manage the businesses. The whole history of the Shaker herb business revolves around a handful of key figures who had the knowledge, commitment, stamina, initiative, and integrity to make it happen. Their names come up again and again: Garrett Lawrence, Barnabus Hinckley, Edward Fowler, Alonzo Hollister, and Benjamin Gates at New Lebanon; Simon Atherton and Elisha Myrick at Harvard; Thomas Corbett and William Tripure at Canterbury; and Peter Boyd at Union Village. The Shakers were a communal society with plenty of willing workers, but the success of their herb enterprises depended heavily on these few leaders.

THE SHAKERS AND PATENT MEDICINES

As Oliver Wendell Holmes, a physician and essayist (and father of the Supreme Court justice by the same name), wrote in 1860, "I firmly believe that if the whole *materia medica*, as now used, could be sunk to the bottom of the sea, it would be all the better for mankind—and all the worse for the fishes." The truth is, conventional doctors were just about empty-handed at that point. Most of the old standbys of heroic medicine had been abandoned, and modern treatments such as antibiotics were still many decades away. But the number of herbal remedies had multiplied to a surfeit, as evidenced by the 356 medicinal plants listed in the New Lebanon catalog in 1851. Were all of those plants really effective? Holmes was skeptical, and so am I. And yet—if only Holmes had known—the situation was going to get even worse, for the next few decades were the heyday of patent medicines. The success of these products had little to do with their medicinal virtues; they were a triumph of marketing. Cute packages, personalized brand names, catchy slogans, clever advertising, sky-high promises, reassuring testimonials—Americans loved it all and came back for more.

The Shakers were already headed in this direction when they prepared special Thomsonian formulas in the 1830s and 1840s. In the 1850s they added a few products designed especially for other doctors and a few nostrums of their own. After the Civil War they devoted most of their effort to producing these modern, packaged herb products rather than the simple dried herbs of yore. It was a profitable opportunity at a time of need, a chance to earn much more income from a smaller amount of raw materials. That was a boon because there were fewer and fewer brethren to do the gardening and more aging sisters who could sit indoors and do the tedious assembly-line work of packaging and labeling.

One source lists a total of eighty proprietary medicines and herb products developed and sold at different Shaker communities—mostly New Lebanon, Canterbury, Harvard, and Union Village—in the late 1800s. Some products had simple names and made simple claims, like the Shaker Hair Restorer ("Gray hair may be honorable, but the natural color is preferable!"), Pain King ("Orders pain out of doors and sees that the command is obeyed!"), and Shaker Vegetable Family Pills ("Operate so gently and surely, yet without straining or distressing the bowels, that

109

no family can afford to be without them. They break up colds and fevers, and do away with bilious disorders").

Others had more impressive names, such as Aromatic Vegetable Cephalic Snuff, Brother Barnabas Hinckley's Compound Concentrated Syrup of Bitter Bugle, and Vegetable Antidyspeptic Restorative Wine Bitters, and made more impressive claims. For example, Corbett's Compound Concentrated Syrup of Sarsaparilla, manufactured at Canterbury from the 1840s to the 1890s, was promoted as "the Great Purifier of the Blood and other Fluids of the Body" and "a Perfect Health Restorer for Dyspepsia, Indigestion, Pale, Thin and Watery Blood, Malaria and Liver Complaint, Weak Nerves, Lungs, Kidneys, and Urinary Organs, Consumption, Emaciation, and Exhaustion of Delicate Females, Nursing Mothers, Sickly Children and the Aged." The label claimed that it relieved "diseases of the Kidneys, Liver, Bladder, Skin and Blood, Scrofula or King's Evil, Scrofulous Swellings or Sores, Cancerous Ulcers, Canker and Canker Humor, Salt Rheum, Syphilitic Humors, Erysipelas, Dropsy, Scurvy, White Swellings, Gout, Gravel, Rheumatism, Neuralgia, Palpitation of the Heart, Female Weakness, General Debility, Fever and Ague, Loss of Appetite, Nervousness and Emaciation."

How could the Shakers sell this stuff with a straight face and a clear conscience? In some cases I think they simply averted their attention and tried to ignore the extravagant claims. But I'll let them speak for themselves regarding Corbett's Sarsaparilla, quoting from *Mary Whitcher's Shaker House-keeper*, which was published in part to promote this product.

> Our Shakers' Sarsaparilla is not a secret or a quack remedy, nor are its ingredients withheld from those who desire to know them. Our claim to superiority is based on the growth, curing and selection of its several roots and berries, and the care with which they are compounded. We cheerfully submit…the ingredients used in the preparation of this great purifying and strengthening medicine, which are the roots of Sarsaparilla [*Aralia nudicaulis*], Dandelion [*Taraxacum officinale*], Yellow Dock [*Rumex crispus*], Mandrake [*Podophyllum peltatum*, now called mayapple], Black Cohosh [*Cimicifuga racemosa*], Garget [*Phytolacca americana*, now called pokeweed], Indian Hemp [*Apocynum cannabinum*], and the berries of Juniper [*Juniperus communis*] and Cubeb

[*Piper cubeba*, a tropical plant related to pepper, whose berries the Shakers imported], united with Iodide of Potassium [a preservative] made by our Society, because we know them to be the best in the vegetable kingdom, and because we carefully select every one according to its power.

Whether or not Corbett's Sarsaparilla could live up to all the claims made on its label, at least the Shakers could attest that they prepared it from pure, top-quality ingredients, primarily herbs with a long history of medicinal use (some are still recognized as potent today, but others have been dismissed).

Most manufacturers of patent medicines were not as conscientious as the Shakers. Some products were shams, mere sugar water with no active ingredients at all. Others were laced with beguiling quantities of opium or alcohol. In the early 1900s the American Medical Association's Council on Pharmacy and Chemistry conducted a study of herbal and patent remedies and denounced many of them. Soon after, when the Pure Food and Drug Act of 1906 required manufacturers to state the amount of alcohol in these remedies and to indicate the presence of any poisonous ingredients, many products were pulled off the market. But by this time the Shakers had already yielded to the competition and discontinued most of their patent medicines.

DAY-TO-DAY OPERATIONS IN THE HERB BUSINESS

In the golden days, the decades from 1820 to 1860, when the Shakers were growing and gathering hundreds of herbs and selling them as simple dried products and liquid extracts, what kind of work was involved? It was seasonal work, peaking between July and September, when most of the herbs were gathered. It was varied work, because there were so many kinds of herbs and several ways of processing them. It was relatively light work, perhaps tedious but requiring little strength or exertion. It was sociable work, occupying groups of children, sisters and brethren, and the elderly. And generally speaking it was popular work, offering a chance to go outdoors in summer and the satisfaction of transforming rough piles of raw materials into tidy stacks of compact, neatly wrapped packages for sale.

The outdoor work started in spring, when the gardeners spread manure and compost and plowed the soil, divided perennials, sowed

111

annuals, and engaged neighboring farmers to grow crops that were in high demand. Throughout the summer the gardeners tried to keep up with hoeing and weeding the herb fields, but their main challenge was processing all the fresh herbs—hauling them in, spreading them out to dry, then gathering them into barrels for storage or getting them ground or pressed. In the fall they cleaned up the garden, made compost piles, and sowed those few seeds that had to winter outdoors.

Most of the "green" herbs were harvested between June and September by picking or cutting whole stems or stalks, or just plucking off the tops. Often sisters and children did this job, gathering just one herb at a time to avoid mixups, and piling them onto linen sheets fifteen feet square. They picked some herbs from the garden, of course, but also traveled around the Shaker properties and out into the neighborhood by horse and wagon, and sometimes even took the train to visit sites where they could gather herbs from the wild. Back at the Shaker village, the sheets of herbs were carried indoors and suspended in the attics or lofts of big buildings to dry, or the fresh-cut herbs were spread to dry on the attic floors, dried in kilns heated by coal or wood fires, or put into the still kettle for distillation.

Barks were gathered from the Shaker woodlands, usually in late May or June just as the trees were leafing out. Roots were usually dug after a few frosts in fall. Sometimes the Shaker men went out to peel bark and dig roots, but often they assigned the job to hired hands or purchased bark and roots (and other herbs, too) from outsiders, including local Native Americans.

From late fall to spring the work was done indoors; the summer's crops of dried herbs were pressed into compact blocks, wrapped, and labeled, and orders were filled. Sometimes the sisters helped with these jobs, and sometimes the men worked alone.

I'll close this chapter with a few words from the Shakers themselves on the jobs of growing, gathering, and processing herbs, but first, I have to say that I have not found answers to some of my questions on this topic. For example, I wonder how they handled aconite, belladonna, and other dangerously poisonous plants without getting hurt. (They didn't have rubber gloves.) I wonder how they processed wormwood, tansy, and other plants with powerful odors without suffering from headaches or dizziness. (Even working outdoors with plenty of fresh air, some herb fumes are strong. Indoors they can be overwhelming.) I wonder how they labeled each batch of gathered herbs, and what they did if the labels got mixed up or lost, as can happen. (Once they're dried and crumbled, most herbs look about the same, and when you're working around them all the time your nose becomes so saturated that they all smell the same too.) And I wonder, once they dried a batch of herbs, how they *kept* them dry. (The Northeast is so humid that dried herbs quickly regain moisture from the air, and they can even mold if they're not sealed in airtight containers.) These all seem like plausible problems, but in what I've read so far, the Shakers don't mention them.

To give you a feeling for the work it involved, here's what they did say about the herb business. These excerpts from the journal of Elisha Myrick at Harvard are arranged by date to show the seasonal progression of work. Elisha's work varied from day to day, and he faced it all with responsibility and relish. Along with the tasks mentioned here, he also did a lot of hoeing and weeding in the summer, and carpentry, plumbing, maintenance work, and tinkering year-round.

January 9, 1850. Work all night packing and making out bills.

January 17, 1850. Up at 4 o'clock putting up herbs to go to Boston. Three sisters pick over dry sage in the evening.

February 14, 1850. After meeting in the evening we got some help and put up 18 dozen large cans of thyme till 12 o'clock.

April 30, 1850. Took up two waggon loads of sage roots and carried them over to John Blanchard to cultivate for us this year. He is to cut it and bring it to us green and after it is dried he is to have seven cents per pound.

May 11, 1850. Sow hollyhock and sweet balm seeds.

May 13, 1850. Sow Jerusalem oak, poppy seed and lavender.

May 14, 1850. Sow dock seed, marshmallow, pennyroyal, peppergrass.

May 17, 1850. Sow 5 rows of poppy seeds.

113

May 18, 1850. Go into the woods to peel white oak bark and find it is too early.

May 24, 1850. Peel white oak bark.

May 30, 1850. Cut 500 lbs. sarsaparilla root and 300 lbs. sage.

June 25, 1850. An Indian came here to buy some herbs.

August 4, 1851. Cut a lot of sweet balm horehound and hyssop and take them up in the herb house garret to make room to spread the poppy leaves. We have such an abundance of poppy and hollyhock flowers that we have to devote the barn garret entirely to them. Pick 4 sheets of poppy leaves.

August 12, 1850. Seven sisters and 4 brethren go out beyond the depot to pick wintergreen, get a small quantity.

August 13, 1851. Set up the still for distilling spearmint.

August 14, 1851. Cut the thyme in the vineyard and got 4 large sheets full. Fill the still with goldenrod.

August 15, 1851. Cut some of the wormwood in the vineyard and fill the still kettle 3 times.

September 2, 1850. Finish cutting the S. Savory at the west hill garden 21 sheets full in all put up three kettels of peach leaves cut the lavender.

September 13, 1850. Send 15 barrels S. Savory to grind and 2 barrels thyme, cut the thorn apple.

September 30, 1850. An Irishman [hired hand] commenced digging dock root yesterday noon at the west hill garden.

October 7, 1850. Cut the remainder of the sage in the garden which pretty much closes the green herb business for this season.

November 1, 1850. Take the dock root out of the kiln and fill it again with the same. Finish chipping the white oak bark, 7 barrels after being chipped.

November 2, 1850. Press yellow dock root all day 311 lbs. papered and 48 more in the press making 359 lbs. in all.

November 11, 1850. A man by the name of Samuel Hoyt from Canada here to sell herbs and roots.

November 22, 1850. Plow and sow the west hill garden with 8 rows belladonna, dock, cicuta, horehound, and pennyroyal seeds for 1851.

November 23, 1851. Carry the waste stalks from behind the herb house to the garden for mulching.

Myrick enjoyed a varied role, but sometimes herb work was dull and tedious, especially for the Shaker sisters who had to pick over the fresh or dried herbs to separate the leaves from the stalks and reject any inferior material. Here's a sample of what one sister wrote in a journal kept at Harvard in 1866:

August 1. The girls iron, picking over herbs, we have a fresh meat stew for dinner.

August 2. Eunice picking hardhack, we do some colouring [dyeing yarn], picking over herbs.

August 3. Picking over herbs, we have some cucumbers.

August 4. Picking over herbs.

August 9. A rainy day, work on herbs, herbs, herbs.

August 11. Picking over herbs.

But another sister, Marcia Bullard, recalling her childhood at New Lebanon, had lovely memories of herbs. After describing the roses and opium poppies, sections I quoted elsewhere in this book, she gave a general summary:

Then there were the herbs of many kinds. Lobelia, Pennyroyal, Spearmint, Peppermint, Catnip, Wintergreen, Thoroughwort, Sarsaparilla and Dandelion grew wild in the surrounding fields.

115

When it was time to gather them an elderly brother would take a great wagonload of children, armed with tow sheets, to the pastures. Here they would pick the appointed herb and, when their sheets were full, drive solemnly home again. In addition to what grew wild we cultivated an immense amount of dandelion, dried the roots and sold it as "chicory." The witch hazel branches were too rough for women and children to handle, so the brethren cut them and brought them into the herb shop where the sisters made them into hamamelis. We had big beds of Sage, Thorn apple, Belladonna, Marigolds and Camomile, as well as Yellow Dock of which we raised great quantities to sell to the manufacturers of a well-known "sarsaparilla." We also made a sarsaparilla of our own and various ointments. In the herb shop the herbs were dried and then pressed into packages by machinery, labeled and sold outside. Lovage root we exported both plain and sugared and the wild flagroot we gathered and sugared, too. On the whole there was no pleasanter work than that in the "medical garden" and "herb shop."

A SAMPLER
OF SHAKER HERBS

*Vegetable substances afford the mildest, most efficient,
and most congenial remedies to the human frame.*

—CONSTANTINE RAFINESQUE, QUOTED IN
THE CANTERBURY SHAKERS' CATALOG OF MEDICINAL PLANTS

THROUGHOUT THE MIDDLE DECADES of the nineteenth century, the Shakers were selling dried leaves, roots, extracts, oils, and other products made from about four hundred species of medicinal herbs. Why did they use so many different kinds of plants?

One explanation is theoretical, or perhaps I should say philosophical. An idea that originated in ancient times and has resurfaced every few centuries since is that for every disease there is a specific remedy. The Thomsonians and Eclectics renovated the idea for nineteenth-century use by adding scores of native American plants to the previous lists of potential remedies. In reading about herbal medicine, you'll come upon two terms from this philosophy: "specific," which means an herb that is considered to cure a specific ailment, and "simple," which means a single herb used by itself.

It's very appealing to think that the Creator has anticipated our needs and supplied a specific remedy for each of our diseases and ailments, but in practice herbal treatments are rarely so straightforward. As Samuel Thomson described the widow Benton's efforts at healing: "When one thing did not produce the desired effect, she would try something else, till [the symptoms] were relieved." Virtually every plant of medicinal value has been prescribed for multiple ailments, and for each ailment different plants have been prescribed. Studying herbal medicine is confusing because there's so much overlap and inconsistency in discussions of which plants are good for what ailments. Catalogs from different Shaker communities often listed the same herbs but cited different properties or uses for them, depending on which books the community chose as references.

I doubt that the Shakers worried about this inconsistency, because they weren't responsible for prescribing or dispensing the herbs. Their business was simply to *produce* what the doctors ordered, and in the mid-1800s doctors were ordering hundreds of different herbs. While the Shakers were very careful about preparing their herbal products— they took care to identify plants with certainty, name them correctly, harvest the proper parts at the appropriate season, dry or process them promptly, avoid contamination, and eliminate inferior material—they certainly didn't do research to test particular herbs and justify the claims made about them. And they didn't necessarily use all these herbs themselves, especially as they started placing more and more emphasis on maintaining good health rather than treating disease.

Now that medicinal herbs are in the news again, people are asking, "Are herbs effective? Are they safe?" The answer may be yes, no, maybe, sometimes, or nobody knows—it varies from case to case. Where appropriate, I'll mention current thinking on some of the Shaker herbs in this chapter. Several have been validated by modern research, and others have been discounted. In general, I urge you to approach herbs with caution. When you're seriously ill, don't read a book—go see a doctor.

I want to emphasize that the Shakers gathered and grew a wide variety of medicinal plants, many more than are included in today's herb gardens. But it's easy to get bogged down in a long alphabetical list, so I've chosen a representative sample of Shaker herbs and grouped them into categories.

CULINARY OR "SWEET" HERBS

Most of the Shaker villages that produced herbs sold cans of four dried culinary or "sweet" herbs: sage, summer savory, sweet marjoram, and thyme. These were used—sparingly, in most cases—to season soups, stews, meat dishes, and other foods. They were used also, and perhaps more commonly, as home remedies.

Sage or common sage (*Salvia officinalis*) is a bushy perennial with gray-green leaves and lovely blue-purple flowers in early summer. Several Shaker villages produced more sage than any other herb;

Hancock, for example, devoted four acres of its ten-acre herb garden to this herb. Although sage is reliably perennial in milder climates, it's only marginally hardy in New England, so the Shaker gardeners often spread mulch or mounded soil over the roots for winter protection, or dug up the roots and stored them in a root cellar. Each spring they divided the roots and planted them out in freshly prepared soil. Treated this way, sage doesn't flower but produces lots of fresh leafy shoots. The Shakers harvested sage repeatedly from June through September, cutting the tops back partway each time. Sage was used as a seasoning and preservative in sausage. Medicinally, a tea brewed from dried sage leaves was (and still is) recommended for coughs, colds, sore throats, fevers, and upset stomachs. The Shakers described sage as a sudorific, an herb that induces perspiration, but today it is considered just the opposite and is used to reduce excessive perspiration.

Summer savory (*Satureja hortensis*) is an annual with narrow green or purplish green leaves and tiny white flowers. A variable plant, it can be slender and erect or branching and bushy. The Shakers planted rows of the tiny seeds in May and harvested the plants by cutting them at ground level just before frost in September. Fresh or dried, the leaves have a sharp, pungent aroma. Summer savory is a traditional seasoning for green or dry beans. The essential oil has been used to relieve toothaches, and *The Gardener's Manual* recommended summer savory tea as "a good remedy for the nervous head ache. Drink it hot just before going to bed."

Sweet marjoram (*Origanum majorana*) is a small, bushy plant with slightly fuzzy gray-green leaves and knotlike clusters of round flowerheads. The plant tops have a delicious spicy aroma. In frost-free regions sweet marjoram is a short-lived perennial, but the Shakers grew it as an annual, sown in late spring and harvested by cutting off the tops in late summer or early fall. Tea brewed from the dried leaves was deemed a stimulant and tonic.

There are many species and hybrids of thyme, but the Shakers primarily grew a species that is commonly called mother-of-thyme or creeping thyme (now labeled *Thymus pulegioides*, but known to the Shakers as *T. serpyllum*). This is a fast-growing, vigorous, hardy perennial that forms a bushy patch of fine twiggy stems, covered with fragrant, shiny, dark green leaves and pinkish purple flowers. Elisha Myrick

119

referred to gathering thyme in the orchard at Harvard, where it probably grew in the grass under and around the trees. Mother-of-thyme tolerates more shade and moisture than most thyme species. It self-sows readily and escaped from the Shaker villages and other early gardens, so it is often seen along roadsides or in fields and lawns in western Massachusetts and adjacent states. The Shakers recommended thyme tea (brewed from the dried tops) for upset stomachs and headaches. Now it is recommended for bronchitis, sore throats, and persistent coughs as well. The essential oil of thyme contains thymol, used today as an antiseptic.

OTHER CULINARY HERBS USED MEDICINALLY

The Shaker medicinal plant catalogs listed many plants that we think of today as culinary herbs. Most of these were sold in dried form.

We regard basil (*Ocimum basilicum*), for example, as an ingredient in pesto and as a seasoning for tomato dishes, but the Shakers used basil tea to allay excessive vomiting. In my experience, basil leaves lose most of their aroma and flavor when dried. I haven't learned that the Shakers knew a way to prevent that. Lemon balm (*Melissa officinalis*) does dry well and makes a pleasant tea, though it smells more lemony than it tastes. People today drink lemon balm tea hot or iced, plain or sweetened, as a beverage; the Shakers recommended drinking it hot to relieve mild fevers. Current research also suggests that repeated swabbing with strong lemon balm tea can dispel cold sores.

Peppermint (*Mentha x piperita*) and spearmint (*M. spicata*) are favorite flavorings for candies, breath fresheners, and toothpastes now. The Shakers distilled these mints to produce flavorings for food and for disagreeable-tasting medicines, and also recommended mint teas for soothing upset stomachs, reducing nausea, and relieving colic.

Many plants in the carrot family (Umbelliferae), including carrots themselves, have fragrant seeds. The Shakers recommended the aromatic and tasty seeds of dill (*Anethum graveolens*), fennel (*Foeniculum vulgare*), coriander (*Coriandrum sativum*), and caraway (*Carum carvi*) for various ailments related to the digestive system—to relieve flatulence, soothe colic, comfort upset stomachs, allay nausea, stimulate the appetite, stop hiccups, and sweeten the breath. The small, crunchy seeds could be chewed or brewed for teas. These plants all have fragrant foliage, too, but generally it was the seeds that were used as remedies. Several other plants in the carrot family were also used medicinally. The Shakers used parsley (*Petroselinum crispum*) in salads and cooking but also recommended a parsley-seed rinse to destroy hair lice, a poultice of crushed parsley leaves to relieve insect bites, and tea brewed from dried parsley root as a diuretic. Various preparations from angelica (*Angelica archangelica*) and lovage (*Levisticum officinale*)—both of which are bold plants with large compound leaves, big flower heads, hollow stems, thick roots, and sweet, spicy aromas—were eaten like candy or used to relieve stomachache, heartburn, and toothache.

Two herbs that we value for their pungent flavor are hot peppers and horseradish. The Shakers listed ground, dried cayenne pepper (*Capsicum annuum*), but they didn't necessarily grow the peppers themselves. Most years the growing season in the Northeast is too cool and short for these peppers to fully ripen, so the Shakers imported them from Africa. Hot-pepper tea was a key element in the Thomsonian program of therapy; it definitely "warms the system." An ointment of hot pepper soaked in vegetable oil or lard was a folk remedy for rheumatism. Horseradish (*Armoracia rusticana*) is a hardy perennial that forms a clump of large, rough, oblong leaves and sends up a tall flower stalk in summer. The Shakers dug the roots in fall and dried them. The pungency of the roots is diminished when they are dried, but it's still enough to make your mouth water. Grated horseradish root boiled in brown-sugar syrup is a traditional cough remedy, and a poultice of the roots has been used externally for rheumatism.

I'll add saffron here to dispel some confusion about it. The "saffron" listed in several Shaker herb catalogs was not true saffron (*Crocus sativus*), a fall-blooming relative of the familiar spring crocus. True saffron prefers hot, dry climates and grows weakly in the Northeast. Oddly it does not set seeds in any climate; it's a sterile plant. What the Shakers grew was safflower, sometimes called American saffron (only because it grows well in America; it's actually native to India). Safflower (*Carthamus tinctorius*) is a fast-growing annual with prickly foliage and orange, thistle-like flowers. The dried flowers are sometimes used as a substitute for true saffron, which is much harder to produce and much more expensive, but safflower only colors food; it doesn't have the tangy flavor of true saffron. The Shakers listed safflower seeds in their garden

121

seed catalogs and sold dried safflower blossoms as a medicinal herb. They described the blossoms as diuretic and stomachic ("giving tone to the stomach"). Some contemporary herbalists recommend safflower preparations for various conditions, but the plant is now grown mostly for its seeds, which yield a popular salad and cooking oil.

VEGETABLES USED IN MEDICINE

Most people are surprised to see lettuce (*Lactuca sativa*) listed in the Shaker medicinal plants catalogs, but there it is. They produced a fluid extract of lettuce because, as William Buchan wrote in 1816:

> This plant, so valuable as an article of diet, abounds with a milky juice which possesses all the characteristic properties of the opium of the shops, and may be procured in sufficient quantity to repay any labor bestowed for this purpose. The laudanum made from the opium of the lettuce increases the pulse in force and frequency...[and allays] chronic rheumatism and colic...diarrhea, cough, etc....Doubtless the plant may be advantageously cultivated for medical purposes, especially as the opium is procured after the period in which the plant is useful for the table.

Constantine Rafinesque wrote that lettuce is "a good topical sedative and a good diet in many diseases, such as hypochondria, nymphomania, consumption, and nervous complaints, producing a propensity to sleep, and allaying pain. The milk of it is easily collected from incisions with a cotton or sponge, and is similar to opium when inspissated. The extract of the whole plant, although less pure, is equivalent, and 24 lbs. of lettuce give 1 lb. of it. The tincture is also equal to that of opium." Along with common garden lettuce, the Shakers occasionally cultivated a species called wild lettuce (*L. virosa*), which was considered more powerful.

The Shakers at various times also offered extracts of tomatoes (described as a laxative), asparagus roots (a diuretic), and rhubarb roots (a potent cathartic).

POISONOUS PLANTS USED IN MEDICINE

It's disturbing to think that a doctor would purposely administer a plant known to be poisonous, but the risk of poisoning is almost always a matter of dosage. When given cautiously in small doses, a particular herb can be exactly what's required to treat a difficult condition, even though the same herb would be fatal if taken carelessly or in excess. The Shakers grew or gathered several particularly potent herbs. These were not home remedies; the Shakers sold them only to qualified doctors and pharmacists.

Three of these critically useful but definitely poisonous plants belong to the notorious nightshade family. Except for its glossy black berries, deadly nightshade or belladonna (*Atropa belladonna*) is an inconspicuous plant, with plain green leaves and small maroon flowers. All parts of the plant are poisonous—even handling the dry leaves can cause a rash. Again, I wonder how the Shakers managed without rubber gloves, but they gathered the leaves somehow in summer and processed an extract that was used as a painkiller and sedative for convulsions, epilepsy, mania, asthma, and whooping cough.

Henbane (*Hyoscyamus niger*) can be an annual or a biennial; in either case, it's a weedy plant with sticky, smelly, jagged-edged leaves and dirty-looking flowers. The article about New Lebanon published in the *American Journal of Pharmacy* in 1852 stated, "Belladonna and hyoscyamus, especially the latter, require a rich deep soil and abundance of strong animal manure. [The Shakers] find henbane a very precarious crop, as when young it is almost impossible to keep it from being destroyed by insects, and some years they have entirely lost it, notwithstanding their best endeavors to protect it." (Many plants in the nightshade family are chewed by insects that have developed an immunity to the poisons.) Under favorable growing conditions, the article noted, henbane can yield "1300 pounds of good extract from an acre of plants." The extract was used by doctors to induce a deep sleep and applied externally to relieve the pains of rheumatism.

Finally the Shakers grew thorn apple or stramonium (*Datura stramonium*), also known as jimsonweed. Thorn apple grows as a weed on sunny vacant lots across North America. It's a fast-growing annual with tough stalks, large, smelly leaves, prickly pods, and very showy white flowers that resemble small trumpets. Elisha Myrick at Harvard described planting thorn apple in mid-June and picking the leaves in mid-September, just before frost. This herb had many uses in nineteenth-century medicine: the leaves were smoked to relieve asthma, the extract was prescribed as a narcotic and sedative for nervous disorders, and an ointment was used for burns and cuts.

Several other poisonous plants were big sellers for the Shakers. They grew monkshood or aconite (*Aconitum napellus*), a hardy perennial with deeply cut leaves and odd-shaped flowers in a vivid shade of blue. The plant is gorgeous, but all parts are very poisonous. The Shakers made an extract from the roots, which was used to reduce fever, slow the pulse, and relieve severe pain. Foxglove (*Digitalis purpurea*) is another dangerous beauty, often grown today for its spikes of thimble-shaped pink-purple or white flowers. The Shakers sold an extract of foxglove leaves for treating heart conditions, dropsy (fluid retention), asthma, and nervous disorders. As with all these high-risk plants, the Shakers cautioned that foxglove and monkshood should be used only by trained physicians.

To an untrained observer, poison hemlock (*Conium maculatum*—the plant that killed Socrates and no relative at all of the gentle hemlock tree, *Tsuga canadensis*) resembles wild carrot, angelica, sweet cicely, and other herbs in the carrot family. One telltale clue is its stale, foul odor—not at all like the pleasant, spicy aroma of these other plants—but you really have to know what you're doing to distinguish friend from foe in this confusing group of plants. The Shakers sold poison hemlock (which they called cicuta) extract for use as a narcotic. Following Rafinesque's observations, the Shakers thought that cicuta was more potent when gathered from the wild rather than cultivated, so each summer a few brethren would go out to collect it. Franklin Barber took time off from the seed garden to "go after cicuta" on July 2, 1842. That year the New Lebanon Shakers gathered eighteen wagon loads of it, extracted 623 gallons of juice, and ended up with 380 pounds of inspissated juice to sell. Whew. It makes me shudder to think of being in the same room with 380 pounds of cicuta juice.

From the late 1850s to the 1930s, the Shakers at New Lebanon produced Norwood's Tincture of Veratrum Viride by arrangement with Dr. Wesley C. Norwood of South Carolina. *Veratrum viride*, commonly called green hellebore or American hellebore, is a perennial native to rich damp soil in cool woodlands or wetlands. One of the first plants to emerge in spring, it has large leaves that are crisply pleated. Dr. Norwood promoted his tincture (produced from the rhizomes) as a versatile sedative, narcotic, and painkiller. Research today suggests it can lower the heart rate and reduce high blood pressure. More typically, though, hellebore was used in the eighteen and nineteenth centuries as a household poison. Dusts or sprays made from the rhizome were used to kill insect pests on crop plants, and hellebore-treated grain was used to bait and poison rats, mice, and crows.

The Shakers grew acres of opium poppies (*Papaver somniferum*), which they called simply poppies. Sister Marcia Bullard described the scene at New Lebanon in the 1850s: "We always had extensive poppy beds and early in the morning, before the sun had risen, the white-capped sisters could be seen stooping among the scarlet blossoms to slit those pods from which the petals had just fallen. Again after sundown they came out with little knives to scrape off the dried juice. This crude opium was sold at a large price and its production was one of the most lucrative as well as the most picturesque of our industries."

Not only did the Shakers make an "opium equivalent" from lettuce, they produced real opium, too, because it was such a useful and valuable product. Opium and one of its derivatives, morphine, are among the best painkillers ever discovered. During the Civil War the New Lebanon Shakers harvested a ten-acre field of poppies to supply opium and morphine for the military doctors. Of course, opium was also abused. Legally available throughout the nineteenth century, it was a very common ingredient in all kinds of patent medicines—mothers knowingly used opium-spiked syrups to calm their children, and many people were quietly addicted to it.

Some Shaker communities grew poppies but didn't harvest the opium by slitting the pods as described above. Instead, they picked and dried the leaves, flower petals, and immature pods. These dried plant parts contained opium but were much weaker and less valuable than the pure sap. Elisha Myrick at Harvard usually harvested poppies in August, as noted in this series of journal entries from 1851: "August 4. Pick 4 sheets of poppy leaves." "August 5. Pick the remainder of the poppy leaves 5 sheets." "August 25. Pick about one half the poppy heads." "August 26. Finish picking the poppy heads." "August 27. Pull up the poppy stalks." "August 29. Burn the poppy stalks."

He didn't say so, but Elisha must have left a few poppy plants in the field so he could collect ripe seeds for sowing the next year's crop.

However, the Shakers didn't sell poppy seeds, and I haven't seen any indication that they used the seeds in breads or other recipes either. (The poppy seeds used in cooking come from this same plant, but they don't contain any opium.)

ROSES

Sister Marcia Bullard, who wrote that "a rose was useful, not ornamental," and that "its mission was to be made into rose-water," explained, "We had only crimson roses as they were supposed to make stronger rose water than the paler varieties. The rose water we sold, of course, and we used in the community to flavor apple pies. It was also kept in store at the infirmary, and although in those days no sick person was allowed to have a fresh flower to cheer him, he was welcome to a liberal supply of rose water with which to bathe his aching head." Rose water was made by covering fresh roses (or just the petals) with plain water and then distilling it. The Shakers also sold rose oil, which is more concentrated than rose water, and dried rose petals.

They grew two kinds of roses, and it's not always clear which kind is being referred to in journal entries or catalog listings. Both have dark pink or crimson flowers that are very fragrant, and both can be used for making rose water and rose oil and for drying. Most modern herbalists agree with William Buchan's assessment that the apothecary rose (*Rosa gallica* 'Officinalis') is more important medicinally. Its petals "have a pleasant astringency" and "their odor is increased by drying." The damask rose (*R. damascena*) is cherished because distilling the petals yields "the most elegant perfume in vegetable nature…a single drop imparts its fragrance throughout the room or dwelling, and suppresses other less agreeable odours." Both the apothecary rose and the damask rose are hardy, old-fashioned shrub roses that bloom once a year, in June.

NATIVE TREES AND SHRUBS WITH MEDICINAL PROPERTIES

The Shakers gathered bark, root bark, leaves, berries, nuts, and other products from dozens of trees and shrubs that grew wild in their woodlands and fields. Most of these materials were remedies that had been discovered by Native Americans, passed along to the early "root and herb" doctors, and promoted by Buchan, Rafinesque, and other writers.

Among the most important of these was the flowering dogwood (*Cornus florida*), a small tree that grows from New England to Texas and is universally cherished for its large white flowers in early spring. Dried bark from the flowering dogwood, and also from the shrubby red-osier dogwood (*C. sericea*), was regarded as the equivalent of cinchona (bark from *Cinchona pubescens*, the source of quinine) for relieving the symptoms of malaria and lowering fevers. As William Buchan wrote, "In whatever form of disease the cinchona has been decidedly serviceable, the [dogwoods] will be found equally so.... If therefore our native productions are adequate to our exigencies let expensive exotics be rejected." Buchan described the properties of dogwood bark and added that the berries of flowering dogwood, which turn glossy red in fall, have "a very bitter taste" and that an "infusion of them in rum or brandy is much esteemed as an agreeable morning bitter." Harvesting the bark kills a tree, but the Shakers used the pale, fine-grained lumber from dogwood to make weaving shuttles, boxes, and other small wooden ware.

The butternut (*Juglans cinerea*), like the related black walnut, bears edible nuts in hard-to-crack shells, and has pungent-scented compound leaves and attractive wood (although butternut boards are medium brown, not dark brown like black walnut). Butternut trees produce a sweet sap that can be tapped in spring and concentrated into a syrup or sugar like maple sugar, but the Shakers primarily used the bark and root bark, which they boiled in water to make an extract. Lossing reported that the New Lebanon Shakers produced 3,000 pounds of butternut root bark extract in 1855, for use in "making Cathartic Syrup and other soothing syrup recipes." They also used butternut roots to dye wool various shades of tan and brown.

Dogwood bark is bitter and butternut bark is cathartic, but slippery elm (*Ulmus rubra*) bark is soothing. Slippery elm trees resemble the famed American elm, but they don't grow as tall and have larger, stiffer leaves with an unusually rough, sandpaper-like texture. The bark can be used fresh, or dried and ground into a floury powder. Either way, when soaked in water, the bark makes a smooth, gooey mucilage. The Canterbury Shakers described their Flour of Slippery Elm as "applicable to a variety of important uses...in all inflammations of the mucous membranes. It is also a pleasant...diet in consumption. As a poultice, it is valuable in burns, scalds, carbuncles, abscesses and all kinds of

127

external inflammations." The Shakers also sold dried barks and bark extracts from many other trees, including white pine, quaking aspen, white oak, sassafras, sweet birch, wild black cherry, and prickly ash.

The Shakers distilled an extract from twigs of witch hazel (*Hamamelis virginiana*) and also sold the dried leaves. According to Rafinesque, the bark extract is excellent for "painful tumors and piles, external inflammations, sore and inflamed eyes," while tea made from the leaves is good for "amennorrhea, bowel complaints, pains in the sides, bleeding of the stomach, &c." They dried leaves of blackberries, dewberries, and raspberries (*Rubus* spp.) to make an astringent tea that was and still is recommended for diarrhea and dysentery. Meadowsweet or steeplebush (*Spiraea tomentosa*) leaves make a pleasant-tasting tea, also used for diarrhea. The spicy-scented twigs, leaves, and berries of spicebush (*Lindera benzoin*) were recommended for treating colds, reducing fevers, and expelling worms. Rafinesque said the berries of sumac (*Rhus glabra* and other species) were good for "dysentery, rheumatism, sore throat, putrid fevers, hemorrhage, gangrene, &c. They have an agreeable acid taste, make a cooling drink. The powdered seeds are used for piles and wounds. The juice removes warts and [treats various skin problems]."

NATIVE WOODLAND WILDFLOWERS AND FERNS

Along with tree barks and other products, the Shakers gathered roots and tops of many wildflowers that grew in their forests. Again, these were all plants whose medicinal properties had been recognized by Native Americans and adopted by white doctors. Some of these wildflowers are uncommon in the woods today, but you can buy them from wildflower nurseries. The Shakers were able to collect all they needed from wild stands and didn't try to cultivate them. The plants described in the following pages are all long-lived perennials that spread by underground runners. If you gather their roots or rhizomes by thinning here and there, leaving plenty behind, the patch soon recovers and refills the opened spots, and can be harvested again a few years later. Apparently the Shakers followed this practice of harvesting for sustainable yield. Other nineteenth-century herbalists sometimes stripped whole patches bare, gleaning every root, until the plants became too scarce to pursue.

Thorn apple or jimsonweed, a weedy plant with beautiful flowers, had many uses in nineteenth-century medicine.

From the late 1850s to the 1930s, the Shakers at New Lebanon produced Norwood's Tincture of Veratrum Viride, using an extract from the rhizomes of this native perennial wildflower.

The Shakers distilled fragrant rose petals to make rose water,
used as a cosmetic, perfume, and flavoring.

Bark from the flowering dogwood tree is a substitute for quinine, used to lower fevers and relieve the symptoms of malaria.

Wild sarsaparilla carpets the ground in many eastern forests. The Shakers gathered its roots to make sarsaparilla extract, promoted as a tonic and cure-all.

The Shakers collected wild ginger (center) and maidenhair fern
(top right) from the woodlands surrounding their villages.

OPPOSITE PAGE:
Black cohosh is a distinctive plant with flower stalks
four to five feet tall. The Shakers gathered its roots.

The dried and powdered roots of pleurisy root or butterfly weed made a popular remedy for respiratory infections.

Joe-Pye-weed was named for an Indian doctor who used the plant to cure typhus and other fevers.

*Button snakeroot has tough, woody roots that were listed
as a remedy for urinary and menstrual disorders.*

Wormwood is a traditional European herb, used to destroy worms and parasites and also to minimize bruises.

*Tea brewed from the leaves of bee balm or Oswego tea
was described as a remedy for upset stomach.*

OPPOSITE PAGE:
*Simple extracts and ointments made from calendula flowers
help heal cuts, scratches, insect bites, and other minor skin wounds.*

138

English valerian, a perennial with very sweet-smelling flowers, provides one of the most effective herbal tranquilizers.

St. Johnswort flowers are yellow, but when you pick them, they stain your fingertips red. When soaked in alcohol or vegetable oil, they make ruby-red lotions that comfort rough skin or minor sores.

OPPOSITE PAGE:
Marshmallow has velvety leaves and flowers like small hollyhocks. Its roots yield a mucilage that helps relieve sore throats.

Burdock is considered a weed today, but the Shakers sold its
seeds, leaves, and roots for use as gentle home remedies.

Elisha Myrick reported digging, washing, cutting, and drying ginger roots each October. He was referring to wild ginger (*Asarum canadense*), a low, creeping plant that forms large patches in rich soil. It has aromatic rhizomes (usually called roots) and velvety, heart-shaped leaves. Rafinesque said, "The whole plant, but particularly the root, has an agreeable aromatic bitterish taste." He recommended the root as a stimulant useful for "melancholy, palpitations, low fevers, convalescence, etc.," and noted that powdered dried ginger leaves "make a fine stimulating snuff...which may be used in all disorders of the head and eyes."

The aromatic root of wild sarsaparilla (*Aralia nudicaulis*) was the chief ingredient in Corbett's Compound Concentrated Syrup of Sarsaparilla, made at Canterbury. Other Shaker villages sold sarsaparilla extracts too. They also sold extracts of spikenard (*A. racemosa*) and dwarf elder (*A. hispida*) roots. Corbett's promotional claims echoed Rafinesque's description of wild sarsaparilla's values, but Rafinesque regarded these three species as equivalent and praised them all: "All the Spikenards or Aralias are popular medical plants....The roots...give a fine flavor to beer....The fresh roots and leaves chewed and applied to wounds, heal them speedily." Extensive patches of wild sarsaparilla carpet eastern woodlands today, spreading like a ground cover. Spikenard and dwarf elder are larger, bushy plants with attractive foliage and conspicuous round clusters of flowers and berries, but they're both uncommon. The few times I've seen them by the roadside I've had to stop the car to identify what they were.

Goldenseal (*Hydrastis canadensis*) was very abundant in colonial days, then was harvested almost to extinction in the 1800s. Today it has recovered enough to be fairly common in some areas. Goldenseal has deeply lobed leaves on stalks about one foot tall and bears small white flowers for a few days in spring and fruits like red raspberries that last for weeks in summer and fall. The stringy roots are bright yellow inside and have a sharp, bitter flavor. They were used to treat sore eyes, mouths, and throats and to relieve upset stomachs.

Maidenhair fern (*Adiantum pedatum*) has particularly lacy leaflets held on unusually stiff, shiny black stalks. Not as delicate as it looks, maidenhair fern spreads by wiry runners to form large dense patches. The Shakers sold dried maidenhair fronds; tea brewed from the fronds was used to relieve coughs and sore throats.

Blue cohosh or squaw root (*Caulophyllum thalictroides*) has blue berries and blue-green foliage. It grows about knee-high and spreads to form a patch. As Rafinesque wrote, "The root [rhizome] is the only part used.... It is sweetish, a little pungent and aromatic... [good for] rheumatism, dropsy, colic, sore throat, cramp, hiccup, epilepsy, hysterics, inflammation of uterus, &c." Peter Smith identified blue cohosh as "the great medicine that the squaws use at the birth of their children," explaining that they drank blue cohosh tea several times a day for two or three weeks before their time. Smith was very impressed with this herb, noting that "its assistance is very special. The great benefit is the state of safety and of speedy and sure recovery that the mother experiences. I believe that it is always safe."

Black cohosh, also called squaw root, black snakeroot, and bugbane (*Cimicifuga racemosa*), is a tall perennial that is popular today for shady or woodland gardens. Peter Smith described it well: "Its stalk is parted regularly into three branches, which support nice leaves at about two feet high, but the stalk that goes to seed is often four or five feet high, strung toward the top with white blossoms, which terminate in a jumble of pods filled with fine seed; adhering to the stool is a great bunch of small black roots. These roots are purgative, make a good bitter when put in spirits, are famous for curing the chronic rheumatism, and strengthen the system when moderately used." The Shakers soaked the roots in alcohol to produce a "Compound Syrup of Black Cohosh" and also included black cohosh in their sarsaparillas.

WILDFLOWERS NATIVE TO SUNNY OPEN PLACES

The Shakers gathered many native wildflowers from meadows, clearings, and open fields and also cultivated some of these plants in gardens. Once again, these plants were all adopted from Native American medicine and promoted by Smith, Rafinesque, and other writers. The examples given here are popular today as flowering perennials for sunny beds and borders.

Pleurisy root (*Asclepias tuberosa*) is usually called butterfly weed today. It forms clumps of leafy stems topped with broad flat clusters of bright orange flowers that attract many kinds of butterflies. Butterfly weed is a kind of milkweed but doesn't have the usual milky sap. When dried, its large, tuberous roots are easily ground into a powder that can be mixed in water and drunk as a tea. This was a very popular remedy for pleurisy, pneumonia, colds, and other respiratory infections because it made breathing easier and relieved chest pains. It was also used to break fevers because, according to Buchan, it displayed the "remarkable power of affecting the skin, inducing general and plentiful perspiration, without heating the body."

Boneset, also called thoroughwort, feverwort, or crosswort (*Eupatorium perfoliatum*), was a panacea to the Indians and settlers. Rafinesque wrote, "It was one of the most powerful remedies of the native tribes for fevers, &c....the only objection to its general use is its nauseous and disagreeable taste." Even as late as 1892, Millspaugh wrote, "There is probably no plant in American domestic practice that has more extensive or frequent use than this. The attic, or woodshed, of almost every country farm house, has its bunch of dried herb hanging, tops downward from the rafters during the whole year, ready for immediate use should some member of the family, or that of a neighbour, be taken with a cold." Boneset has pairs of gray-green leaves that join at the base, surrounding the stem. It forms clumps of erect leafy stalks topped with loose flat clusters of chalky white flowers. Joe-Pye-weeds (*E. maculatum* and *E. purpureum*) resemble boneset but have leaves in whorls of four to six and pinkish or magenta flowers. Rafinesque wrote, "Joe Pye or gravel root has the same properties as boneset and has been used in fevers and gravel [kidney and bladder stones]. The name Joe Pye is given to it from an Indian of that name, who cured typhus with it, by copious perspiration." The Shakers sold the dried and chopped tops of these plants.

Button snakeroot, gayfeather, devil's bit, or blazing star (*Liatris spicata*) is a striking plant shaped like a large pincushion, with stiff flower stalks that project from a basal tuft of grassy leaves. The stalks are lined with fluffy purple flowers that open first at the tip and proceed downward over a span of several weeks. The Shakers dug and dried the tough, woody roots (sometimes called "bulbs" in today's nursery catalogs) and listed them as a remedy for urinary and menstrual disorders.

Oswego tea or bee balm (*Monarda didyma*) is another striking plant. It spreads quickly, especially in damp soil, to form a big patch of leafy stems topped with moplike clusters of scarlet flowers. The leaves have a pleasantly pungent aroma, but they smell better than they taste. Sometimes Oswego tea was drunk as a substitute for real tea, but the Shakers sold the dried leaves as a remedy for upset stomach, vomiting, and flatulence. Wild bergamot (*M. fistulosa*), a related species, has lavender-pink flowers and a minty aroma; it prefers dry soil. It was used as a tea for colds, headaches, and upset stomachs. Horsemint (*M. punctata*) has an even stronger but quite pleasant aroma. Its very showy spikes are crowded with jagged lavender bracts and dotted yellow flowers. The leaves were also used for tea, but Peter Smith added that horsemint leaves were "famous for raising sweat wherever a bunch of them is applied to the skin, and by that means give ease of pain in any part where they are applied. The same application will merit a trial in any inflammations on the skin, or more deeply seated in any part of your body."

Thimbleweed or coneflower *(Rudbeckia laciniata)* is a carefree, long-lived perennial with bright yellow flowers in late summer. Near old or abandoned farmhouses in the Northeast you often see patches of 'Golden Glow', an old-fashioned cultivar with double flowers. The Shakers listed dried thimbleweed tops as a diuretic and published this account of the herb in the 1837 catalog from Watervliet: "In wasting diseases of the kidneys, this plant has proved an excellent medicine. It is diuretic and balsamic. Its properties were first learned by noticing its effects on a sheep that had lost the use of its hind legs. This animal daily dragged itself to this plant, and ate of it, when to the astonishment of all who noticed its situation, it recovered. By shepherds and herdsmen it has since been used with happy effects in stranguary [painful urination] and similar diseases. It is given in decoction, without much nicety as to dose."

TRADITIONAL EUROPEAN HERBS
THAT ARE STILL PLANTED TODAY
The Shakers sold several herbs that have a long history in European herbalism. These were brought to America by the early settlers (along with the culinary herbs listed above, which are also European) and are commonly planted in herb gardens today. Sometimes you see them growing wild along roadsides and in vacant lots.

148

Wormwood (*Artemisia absinthium*) has finely divided gray-green leaves with a silky texture and bitter aroma. In the early twentieth century, wormwood was notorious as the active ingredient in the narcotic beverage absinthe. Buchan wrote that wormwood "is used in stomach complaints, and is of great service to hypochondriacs.... The essential oil is used both externally and internally for destroying worms....If the plant be macerated in boiling water, and repeatedly applied to a bruise...it will not only speedily remove the pain, but also prevent the swelling and discolouration." Mugwort (*A. vulgaris*) resembles wormwood, but its more coarsely cut leaves are dark green above and white below. Rafinesque wrote that "the leaves, tops and seeds" are "useful in hysterics, spasms, palpitations of the heart, worms, &c." Tansy (*Tanacetum vulgare*), another plant with deeply divided leaves and a strong, pungent aroma, was also used to expel worms. The Shaker catalogs regularly listed dried tops and extracts of these herbs, but the use of all three is discouraged today.

Three more herbs that the Shakers listed for treating bruises, cuts, insect stings, and skin sores are arnica (*Arnica montana*), calendula or pot marigold (*Calendula officinalis*), and St. Johnswort (*Hypericum perforatum*). Arnica is an adaptable, spreading perennial with fuzzy stems and leaves that have a slightly fetid smell. In early summer it bears flowers that look like motheaten dandelions. The Shakers sold extracts of the flowers, made with water or alcohol. Arnica is recommended for external use only. Calendula is an annual often grown for its cheery yellow-orange flowers. The Shakers described calendula as a potherb, and I suppose some people ate the flowers, but more often they were boiled in water, soaked in alcohol, or simmered in melted lard to make washes or ointments for external use on minor wounds. Such home-made calendula remedies are still considered effective. St. Johnswort is a hardy perennial that forms erect clumps or small patches, often growing on roadsides or in pastures. Its fluffy little flowers are bright yellow, but when you pick them, they stain your fingertips red, and when soaked in alcohol or vegetable oil, the flowers make rich red lotions that comfort rough skin or sore spots. St. Johnswort can be taken internally. Rafinesque wrote that a "tea of the leaves gives relief in diseases of the breast and lungs...and for diarrhea, amenorrhea, hysterics, hypochondria, mania, and low spirits." Recent research supports the use of St. Johnswort tea as an antidepressant.

Another Shaker herb that is still considered a safe and effective tranquilizer and sedative is English valerian, valerian, or garden heliotrope (*Valeriana officinalis*). English valerian is sometimes grown in perennial borders because it has nice ferny foliage and intensely sweet-scented flowers. Unfortunately its roots, which are the effective part, smell like dirty socks. For decades the Shakers at Enfield, New Hampshire, produced Brown's Extract of English Valerian (named for Brother Samuel Brown), which they promoted as the "best remedy yet discovered for the cure of Nervousness, Lowness of Spirits, Debility, Hypochondria, Neuralgia, Hysteria, Restlessness, Tic Douloureux, Sick Headache, and every other disease arising from mental affection and nervous exhaustion....It is also an invaluable remedy for outward application, in all cases of Cuts, Bruises, Sores, Sprains, Scalds, Burns, Lameness, Skin Diseases, and every affection requiring external treatment."

Marshmallow (*Althaea officinalis*) resembles hollyhock but has much smaller flowers in shades of pale lavender, pink, or white. Its leaves and stems are so densely covered with velvety white hairs that the plant looks gray rather than green. A hardy perennial, marshmallow grows wild in marshes but thrives in average garden soil too. Buchan wrote, "Every part of the marshmallow, and especially the root, upon boiling, yields a copious mucilage; on account of which it is frequently employed for asthma and hoarseness. Chewed, it is said to afford relief in difficult teething." Marshmallow mucilage was combined with sugar syrup to make the original marshmallow candies. The Shakers sold both dried roots and dried leaves of marshmallow.

MEDICINAL PLANTS THAT WE CALL WEEDS
Some of the medicinal herbs that early colonists brought from Europe became established as weeds in this country so quickly that later settlers assumed they were native plants. Even botanists in the 1800s disagreed whether mullein, clover, plantain, burdock, dock, dandelion, and other now-universal weeds were here before the Europeans came. For example, Eaton regarded mullein as native: "When botanists are so infatuated with wild theory as to tell us the mullein was introduced, they give our youngest pupils occasion to sneer at their teachers." The fact that Native American healers quickly developed their own uses for these plants added to the confusion, but now most botanists agree that all these

plants were introduced after 1492. Although they are generally berated as weeds today, the Shakers both gathered and grew several of these plants, and sold them by the ton.

Burdock (*Arctium lappa*) is a coarse perennial with long stringy roots, giant rhubarb-like leaves, and tough stalks with round burs that stick to your clothes and to your dog's fur. (It's said that these burs were the inspiration for Velcro.) The Shakers sold burdock seeds, leaves, and roots. Buchan described the seeds as a diuretic, the leaves as a poultice for irritated or itchy skin, and the roots as a cathartic, noting that all parts "act without irritation" and could safely be used even for acute disorders.

Yellow dock (*Rumex crispus*), another coarse weed, has large oblong leaves and many stiff, erect stalks that bear thousands of tiny greenish yellow flowers. These ripen into papery-winged fruits carrying dark brown seeds. Dock develops a substantial root system, with a central taproot and several side forks, all bright yellow inside. Elisha Myrick reported sowing dock seeds at Harvard in May and digging the roots in November—it isn't clear whether these were roots from the same year's planting, or from the previous year's. They can be dug either way. The Harvard Shakers were mere dabblers in dock root, though, selling only a few hundred pounds a year. The Shakers at Enfield, New Hampshire, took the prize for this crop: in 1889, they sold 44,000 pounds of dried dock root (worth $22,000) to J. C. Ayer and Co. of Lowell, Massachusetts. That company used the roots in a "sarsaparilla" syrup (dock was also an ingredient in the Shaker sarsaparilla recipes). That's a lot of dock roots—at least five acres' worth, I'd estimate. What else was dock used for? Millspaugh wrote, "The root has been used in medicine from ancient times, as a mild astringent tonic, laxative, and [cleanser]. An ointment of the powdered root with lard [is] a specific for the cure of itch.... Rumex is also considered an excellent dentifrice, especially where the gums are spongy. As a pot-herb the young leaves are well known. The acid [from the roots] is a valuable agent for destroying parasites of the skin." Dock root is used only as a laxative today.

Finally, the familiar dandelion (*Taraxacum officinale*), known to one and all as a weed—or is it an herb? The Shakers ate dandelion leaves as a spring green and brewed a coffee substitute from the dried ground roots. More important, they sold thousands of pounds of dried roots

151

and root extract as remedies for stomach, liver, and digestive ailments and also used the root extract in their Eclectic Liver Pills, designed to "purify the blood." To collect enough roots, the Shakers actually cultivated dandelions as a crop, sowing the seeds in June and digging the roots in fall. But don't be too quick to look out in your lawn and see dollar signs where the dandelions grow. Herbalists today dismiss dandelion products as too weak to be effective remedies.

NOTES

Who Were the Shakers?

p. 9 The "nine cardinal virtues" are as listed in Charles Edson Robinson, *The Shakers and Their Homes* (Somersworth, N.H.: New Hampshire Publishing Co., in collaboration with the Shaker Village in Canterbury, N.H., 1976), pp. 32–33.

p. 15 Other books tell the larger history: An excellent overview of Shaker history is Stephen J. Stein, *The Shaker Experience in America* (New Haven: Yale University Press, 1992). Other good general references are Deborah E. Burns, *Shaker Cities of Peace, Love, and Union* (Hanover, N.H.: University Press of New England, 1993); Priscilla J. Brewer, *Shaker Communities, Shaker Lives* (Hanover, N.H.: University Press of New England, 1986); and June Sprigg, *By Shaker Hands* (New York: Knopf, 1975).

p. 15 Today seven Shakers still live at Sabbathday Lake: Photos and descriptions of the herb industry at Sabbathday Lake are included in Steven Foster, *Herbal Bounty!* (Salt Lake City: Peregrine Smith Books, 1984). Foster, a specialist in medicinal plants, lived and worked with the Sabbathday Lake Shakers in the early 1970s. Another view of the Sabbathday community is presented in Gerard C. Wertkin, *The Four Seasons of Shaker Life: An Intimate Portrait of the Community at Sabbathday Lake* (New York: Simon and Schuster, 1986).

The Shaker Approach to Gardening

p. 17 "Men and women who had turned their eyes": Marguerite Fellows Melcher, *The Shaker Adventure* (Princeton, N.J.: Princeton University Press, 1941), p. 122.

p. 17 *The Gardener's Manual:* The full title of this pamphlet is *The Gardener's Manual; Containing Plain Instructions for the Selection, Preparation and Management of a Kitchen Garden: with practical directions for the cultivation and management of some of the most useful culinary vegetables.* Throughout this book I quote from the 1843 edition, originally published by the Shakers at New Lebanon, N.Y., and reprinted in facsimile by Hancock Shaker Village in 1991.

pp. 18–19 Journal entries note these group efforts: Sally Bushnell, *Journal of work performed by the Sisters at New Lebanon, commencing January 1, 1848.* "All hands turn out": William Trio, *Journal of Farm Work, New Lebanon, commencing April, 1820.*

p. 19 "The utmost neatness is conspicuous": Quoted in Amy Bess Miller, *Shaker Herbs: A History and a Compendium* (New York: Clarkson N. Potter, 1976), p. 24.

p. 21 Early Shakers were probably familiar: Throughout this book I quote from the original edition of Samuel Deane, *The New England Farmer* (Worcester, Mass., 1797).

p. 24 The Shakers "looked upon the soil": Hepworth Dixon, *New America* (London: Hurst and Blackett, 1867), quoted in Edward Deming Andrews, *The People Called Shakers* (New York: Oxford University Press, 1953; reprint, Dover, 1963), p. 116.

p. 27 "This morning I have spent": Quoted in Andrews, *The People Called Shakers*, p. 118.

p. 31 "Forty years ago it was contrary": Sister Marcia Bullard, "Shaker Industries," *Good Housekeeping*, July 1906, pp. 33–37.

Shaker Ideas for Today's Kitchen Garden

p. 50 "a family of five": "Victory Gardens," supplement to *The New Garden Encyclopedia* (New York: William H. Wise & Co., 1944).

p. 55 "The soil for a hot-bed": Franklin Barber, *Journal*, April 13, 1843.

Shaker Vegetables and Vegetable Seeds

p. 59 The business grew quickly: The names, dates, statistics, and other facts on the Shaker seed industry and their competitors are from Edward Deming Andrews, *The Community Industries of the Shakers* (Albany: University of the State of New York, 1933); Faith Andrews, *Work and Worship* (Greenwich, Conn.: New York Graphic Society, 1974); Burns, *Shaker Cities of Peace, Love, and Union*; and Margaret Frisbee Sommer, *The Shaker Garden Seed Industry* (Old Chatham, N.Y.: Shaker Museum Foundation, 1972).

Information about nineteenth-century agriculture and vegetables was drawn from Robert F. Becker, "Vegetable Gardening in the United States: A History, 1565–1900," *HortScience* 19, no. 5 (October 1984); Fearing Burr, Jr., *Garden Vegetables and How to Cultivate Them* (Boston, 1866); U. P. Hedrick, *A History of Horticulture in America to 1860* (New York: Oxford University, 1950); U. P. Hedrick, *Sturtevant's Notes on Edible Plants* (Report of the New York State Agricultural Experiment Station for 1919); Howard S. Russell, *A Long, Deep Furrow: Three Centuries of Farming in New England* (Hanover, N.H.: University Press of New England, 1976); and Mme. Wilmorin-Andrieux, *The Vegetable Garden* (London: John Murray, 1885; reprint, Jeavons-Leler Press, 1976).

p. 61 "by reason of others as well as ourselves": Franklin Barber, *Journal*, April 26, 1841.

p. 62 Typical journal entries tally the work: Entries in this section are all from the *Journal of Garden Accounts, New Lebanon, 1840–1849.*

p. 63 It's not that raising seeds is difficult: My references on seed production include Robert Johnston, Jr., *Growing Garden Seeds: A Manual for Gardeners and Small Farmers,* 2nd ed. (Albion, Me.: Johnny's Selected Seeds, 1983); Oscar A. Lorenz and Donald N. Maynard, *Knott's Handbook for Vegetable Growers,* 3rd ed. (New York: Wiley-Interscience, 1988); and *Seeds: The Yearbook of Agriculture for 1961* (Washington: U.S. Department of Agriculture, 1961).

p. 65 "all Cabbages will mix": Amelia Simmons, *The First American Cookbook,* a facsimile of the original 1796 edition of *American Cookery* (New York: Dover, 1984), p. 14. All subsequent quotes are from this edition.

p. 68 *Mary Whitcher's Shaker House-keeper* (Canterbury, N.H., 1882; facsimile reprint, Hancock Shaker Village, 1972).

The Shaker Medicinal Plant Industry

p. 97 Starting about 1820 and continuing: My references for this paragraph and subsequent sections include Miller, *Shaker Herbs*; Galen Beale and Mary Rose Boswell, *The Earth Shall Blossom: Shaker Herbs and Gardening* (Woodstock, Vt.: Countryman Press, 1991); Edward Deming Andrews and Faith Andrews, "Herb Lore," in *Fruits of the Shaker Tree of Life* (Stockbridge, Mass.: Berkshire Traveller Press, 1975), pp. 30–40; and Faith Andrews, "Medicinal Herbs," in *Work and Worship: The Economic Order of the Shakers* (Greenwich, Conn.: New York Graphic Society, 1974), pp. 63–74.

p. 98 Facing problems like that: My references for the discussion of nineteenth-century medicine include Morris Fishbein, *Fads and Quackery in Healing* (New York: Covici, Friede Publishers, 1932); Barbara Griggs, *A History of Herbal Medicine* (New York: Viking, 1981); and Lester S. King, M.D., *The Medical World of the Eighteenth Century* (Chicago: University of Chicago Press, 1958).

p. 102 "roots and herbs, applied," "This plant is what I have called," and subsequent quotes from Samuel Thomson are from *A Narrative of the life and medical discoveries of Samuel Thomson; containing an account of his system of practice* (Boston, 1822; reprint, Arno Press, 1972).

p. 103 "The handwritten volumes": J. Worth Estes, "The Shakers and Their Proprietary Medicines," *Bulletin of the History of Medicine* 65 (1991), p. 164.

p. 104 The earliest Shakers: My references for Shaker methods of healing themselves include Andrews, *The People Called Shakers*; Melcher, *The Shaker Adventure*; Stein, *The Shaker Experiment in America*; and Anna White and Leila S. Taylor, *Shakerism, Its Meaning and Message* (Columbus, Ohio, 1904; reprint, New York: AMS Press Reprint, 1971).

p. 109 One source lists a total: The patent medicines are listed in the appendix to Estes, "The Shakers and their Proprietary Medicines," pp. 182–84.

p. 115 "Then there were the herbs": Bullard, "Shaker Housekeeping," *Good Housekeeping*, July 1906, p. 33.

A Sampler of Shaker Herbs

p. 118 I've chosen a representative sample: Information, quotes, and comments on the listings in Shaker catalogs come from the catalogs themselves, as seen in the library at Hancock Shaker Village and the Case-Western Reserve microfilm collections of Shaker documents; and from Miller, *Shaker Herbs*; and Beale and Boswell, *The Earth Shall Blossom*.

      Quotes and comments on the traditional and nineteenth-century uses of herbs are from William Buchan, M.D., *Every man his own doctor; or, a treatise on the prevention and cure of diseases, by regimen and simple medicines. To which is added, a Treatise on the Materia Medica, in which the medicinal qualities of indigenous plants are given and adapted to common practice* (New Haven: Nathan Whiting, 1816); Peter Smith, *The Indian Doctor's Dispensatory* (Cincinnati, 1813); Constantine S. Rafinesque, *Medical Flora, or Manual of the Medical Botany of the United States in North America*, 2 vols. (Philadelphia: Atkinson-Alexander, 1828, 1830); Charles F. Millspaugh, *American Medicinal Plants* (1892; reprint, New York: Dover, 1974); and Charlotte Erichsen-Brown, *Use of Plants for the Past 500 Years* (Aurora, Ont.: Breezy Creeks Press, 1979).

      Information on the appearance, cultivation, and naming of herbs was written in conformation with Rita Buchanan, ed., *Taylor's Guide to Herbs* (Boston: Houghton Mifflin, 1995); and Steven Foster and James A. Duke, *A Field Guide to Medicinal Plants: Eastern and Central North America* (Boston: Houghton Mifflin, 1992). Information on the contemporary uses of medicinal herbs was drawn from these two books and also from Penelope Ody, *The Complete Medicinal Herbal* (New York: Dorling Kindersley, 1993); Varro Tyler, *Herbs of Choice* (Binghamton, N.Y.: Pharmaceutical Products Press, 1994); and Varro Tyler, *The Honest Herbal: A Sensible Guide to the Use of Herbs and Related Remedies*, 3rd. ed. (Binghamton, N.Y.: Pharmaceutical Products Press, 1993).

p. 124 To an untrained observer: The Shakers used the common name cicuta for *Conium maculatum,* a European herb that had been introduced to this country. They did not gather the native plant *Cicuta maculata,* commonly called water hemlock.

p. 125 "We always had extensive poppy beds": Bullard, "Shaker Housekeeping," p. 33.

p. 150 "When botanists are so infatuated": Amos Eaton, *Manual of Botany for the Northern and Middle States of America, containing generic and specific descriptions of the indigenous plants and common cultivated exotics, growing north of Virginia,* 3rd. ed. (Albany, 1822), p. 180.

NOTES

Shaker communities and their living history museums welcome visitors.
Hancock Shaker Village, Pittsfield, Massachusetts; Shakertown at Pleasant Hill,
Harrodsburg, Kentucky; Canterbury Shaker Village, Canterbury,
New Hampshire; Shakertown, South Union, Kentucky;
and Mount Lebanon Shaker Village, New Lebanon, New York,
all have exhibits that show the history of Shaker gardening.
The United Society of Shakers, Sabbathday Lake, Maine, has working
vegetable and herb gardens and orchards that demonstrate its
continuing agricultural industry as well as historic exhibits.

INDEX